PORTABLE CHEF

Low Fat

Kathryn Hawkins

SMITHMARK

This edition published in 1998 by SMITHMARK Publishers,
a division of U.S. Media Holdings Inc.,
115 West 18th Street, New York, NY 10011.

SMITHMARK books are available for bulk purchase for sales promotion
and premium use. For details write or call the manager of special sales,
SMITHMARK Publishers, 115 West 18th Street, New York, NY 10011.

Produced by Haldane Mason, London

Acknowledgments
Art Director: Ron Samuels
Editorial Director: Sydney Francis
Managing Editor: Jo-Anne Cox
Design: dap ltd
Photography: Iain Bagwell
Home Economist: Kathryn Hawkins
Nutritional information: Anne Sheasby and Annette Yates

ISBN: 0-7651-0877-1

Printed in China

10 9 8 7 6 5 4 3 2 1

Note
Unless otherwise stated, milk is assumed to be full fat, eggs are medium,
and pepper is freshly ground black pepper. The calorie counts and fat content analysis
do not include the serving suggestions.

Contents

Introduction

No one who has more than a passing interest in their health can be unaware of the problems associated with a diet that contains too much fat. A high level of fat consumption is implicated in obesity—and all that that entails—coronary disease, diabetes, and even cancer. The message that we should all cut down on the fat in our diets is reinforced every time we go shopping, and it is almost impossible to walk around a supermarket without being beset on all sides by labels proclaiming low-fat this, reduced-fat that, and no-fat the other.

Cutting the amount of fat in our diets is, of course, an effective way to lose weight, simply because it will reduce the number of calories we consume, as well as reducing the likelihood that we will contract a serious disease. However, before we cut fat out of our lives completely, it is important to remember that we all need to include a certain amount of fat in our daily intake of food if our bodies are to function properly. Essential fatty acids are needed to build cell membranes and for other vital bodily functions. Our brain tissue, nerve sheaths, and bone marrow need fat, for example, and we all need fat to protect vital organs, such as our liver, kidneys, and heart.

Nutritionists suggest that we should aim to cut our intake of fat to 27-30 percent of our total daily calorie intake. If your average diet totals 2,000 calories, this will mean eating no more than approximately 2¾ ounces of fat a day. As a guide, bear in mind that most people consume about 40 percent of their daily calories in the form of fat. Remember, however, that if you are being treated for any medical condition, you must discuss with your doctor or other professional the changes you propose making in your diet before you begin your new regime.

When you are thinking about reducing your intake of fat, it is important to know that fats can be broadly divided into saturated and unsaturated fat. Saturated fats are those that are solid at room temperature, and they are found mainly in animal products—butter and cheese, high-fat meats (sausages, pâté, fatty bacon), cakes, chocolate, potato chips, cookies, coconut, and hydrogenated (hardened) vegetable or fish oils. Unsaturated fats are healthier—but they are still fats. Your target should be a reduction to 8 percent of your daily calories in the form of saturated fats, with the remainder in the form of unsaturated fats. These are usually liquid at room temperature and come from vegetable sources—olive oil, peanut oil, sunflower oil, safflower oil, and corn oil. Remember, though, that oil is only another name for liquid fat. Using oil instead of margarine or butter to fry onions or garlic will do nothing to reduce your overall intake of fat.

INGREDIENTS

One of the simplest and most beneficial changes you can make in your diet is to change from full-fat milk, cream, cheese, and yogurt to a low- or reduced-fat equivalent. Low-fat milk, for example, has all the nutritional benefits of whole milk, but only ⅓ ounce of fat per 2½ cups, compared with ¾ ounce of fat per 2½ cups in whole milk. Use skim milk to make custards and sauces and you will not notice the difference in flavor. Low-fat yogurt mixed with chopped chives is a delicious and healthy alternative to butter or soured cream.

Most vegetables are naturally low in fat and can be used to make a meal of meat or fish go further. Recent nutritional research indicates that we should all aim to eat five portions of fresh fruit and vegetables every day because they contain what are known as antioxidant vitamins, including beta carotene (which creates vitamin A in the body), and vitamins C and E. The antioxidant vitamins in vegetables are thought to help prevent a number of degenerative illnesses (including cancer, heart diseases, arthritis, and even ageing of the skin) and to protect the body from the harmful effects of pollution and ultraviolet light, which can damage the body's cells. Phytochemicals, which occur naturally in plants, are thought to be instrumental in the fight against cancer.

Steaming is the best way to cook vegetables to preserve their goodness. Boiling can, for example, destroy up to three-quarters of the vitamin C present in green vegetables. If you have to boil, cook the vegetables as quickly as possible and avoid over-cooking, which also destroys the carotene.

It is a good idea to make your own stock to use as the basis of casseroles and soups. The ready-made stocks and stock cubes that are available from stores are often high in salt and artificial flavorings. Instead, use fresh herbs and spices in the water in which vegetables have been cooked. Liquids in which meat and fish of various kinds have been cooked should be saved, too. Chill the liquid in the refrigerator and you will be able to remove and discard the fat, which will have risen to the top of the container and solidified.

Pasta, noodles, legumes, and grains can all be used in the low-fat diet, and they are useful for bulking out dishes. Pasta is available in a wide range of shapes, and helps to boost your carbohydrate intake. Inadequate intake of carbohydrates can result in fatigue and poor energy levels. Whole wheat pasta is also high in fiber, which helps to speed the passage of waste material through the digestive system. Stir cooked brown rice into soups and casseroles to thicken them, or mix one part red lentils with three parts lean ground beef to make a smaller amount go further. Check that noodles and pasta have not been enriched with egg—look for whole wheat or rice varieties.

EQUIPMENT

Good quality nonstick pans and cookware will directly reduce the amount of fat needed for cooking, and are easier to clean. Use plastic implements or wooden spoons with nonstick pans so that you do not scratch the surface.

A ridged skillet makes it possible to cook with the minimum amount of fat or oil, because the fat drips down between the ridges rather than being absorbed by the food. When you are stir-frying, use the smallest possible amount of oil. Keep the heat constant and the food moving to ensure quick, even cooking. Use a nonstick wok, which will help you cut down still further on the amount of oil you need.

Use a perforated spoon to remove food from the skillet, so that cooking juices—particularly fats—are left behind. Absorbent paper towels are useful for draining surface oil and fat from food that has just been cooked, but they can also be used to mop up fat that rises to the top during cooking. Use plain, unpatterned paper towels so that no dye is transferred to the food.

Soups & Starters

Many favorite snacks and starters—especially those that we buy ready-prepared on supermarket shelves and in cans—are surprisingly high in fat. Next time, before you buy, think instead about making some of the appetizing recipes on the following pages—they will get your meal off to a wonderful low-fat start.

Soups are a traditional first course, but, served with crusty bread, they can also be a satisfying meal in their own right. Although it does take a little longer, consider making your own stock by using the liquid left after cooking vegetables, and the juices from fish and meat that have been used as the base of casseroles. Use a potato to thicken your soups, rather than stirring in the traditional thickener of flour and water—or, worse, flour and fat.

If you want a change from soup, try a few starters, such as a light Cheesy Ham and Celery Savory or Parsleyed Chicken and Ham Pâté served with a refreshing salad, or flavor-filled Spinach Cheese Molds.

Chicken & Asparagus Soup

Serves 4 • CALORIES PER SERVING: 236 • FAT CONTENT PER SERVING: 2.9 G

INGREDIENTS

8 ounces fresh asparagus
3³/₄ cups fresh chicken stock
²/₃ cup dry white wine
1 sprig each fresh parsley, dill,
  and tarragon

1 garlic clove
¹/₃ cup vermicelli rice noodles
12 ounces lean cooked
  chicken, finely shredded

salt and white pepper
1 small leek

1 Wash the asparagus and trim away the woody ends. Cut each spear into pieces about 1½ inches long.

2 Pour the stock and wine into a large saucepan and bring to a boil.

3 Wash the herbs and tie them with clean string. Peel the garlic clove and add, with the herbs, to the saucepan, together with the asparagus and noodles. Cover and simmer for 5 minutes.

4 Stir in the chicken and plenty of seasoning. Simmer gently for a further 3–4 minutes until heated through.

5 Using a sharp knife, trim the leek, slice it down the center, and wash under running water to remove any dirt. Shake dry and shred finely.

6 Remove the herbs and garlic from the pan and discard. Ladle the soup into warm bowls, sprinkle with shredded leek, and serve at once.

VARIATION

You can use any of your favorite herbs in this recipe, but choose those with a subtle flavor so that they do not overpower the asparagus. Small, tender asparagus spears give the best results and flavor.

COOK'S TIP

Rice noodles contain no fat and are an ideal substitute for egg noodles.

Beef, Water Chestnut, & Rice Soup

Serves 4 • CALORIES PER SERVING: 205 • FAT CONTENT PER SERVING: 4.5 G

INGREDIENTS

12 ounces lean beef (such as rump or sirloin)
4 cups fresh beef stock
1 cinnamon stick, broken
2 star anise
2 tbsp dark soy sauce
2 tbsp dry sherry

3 tbsp tomato paste
4 ounce can water chestnuts, drained and sliced
3 cups cooked white rice
1 tsp zested orange rind
6 tbsp orange juice
salt and pepper

TO GARNISH:
strips of orange rind
2 tbsp snipped chives

1 Using a sharp knife, carefully trim away any fat from the beef. Cut the beef into thin strips and then place into a large saucepan.

2 Add the stock, cinnamon, star anise, soy sauce, sherry, tomato paste, and water chestnuts. Bring to a boil, skimming away any surface film with a flat ladle. Cover the pan and simmer gently for about 20 minutes or until the beef is tender.

3 Skim the soup with a flat ladle again to remove any film. Remove and discard the cinnamon and star anise and blot the surface with absorbent paper towels to remove any fat.

4 Stir in the rice, orange rind, and juice. Adjust the seasoning if necessary. Heat through for 2–3 minutes before ladling into warm bowls. Serve garnished with orange rind and snipped chives.

VARIATION

Omit the rice for a lighter soup that is an ideal starter for a Chinese meal of many courses. For a more substantial soup that would be a meal in its own right, add diced vegetables such as carrot, bell pepper, corn, or zucchini.

Winter Beef & Vegetable Soup

Serves 4 • CALORIES PER SERVING: 161 • FAT CONTENT PER SERVING: 3.3 G

INGREDIENTS

1/3 cup pearl barley	1 large carrot, diced	salt and pepper
5 cups fresh beef stock	1 leek, shredded	2 tbsp fresh parsley, chopped,
1 tsp dried mixed herbs	1 medium onion, chopped	to garnish
8 ounces lean rump or sirloin	2 celery stalks, sliced	crusty bread, to serve
beef		

---

1 Place the pearl barley in a large saucepan. Pour in the stock and add the mixed herbs. Bring to a boil, cover, and simmer for 10 minutes.

2 Meanwhile, trim any fat from the beef and cut the meat into thin strips.

3 Skim away any scum that has risen to the top of the stock with a flat ladle.

4 Add the beef, carrot, leek, onion, and celery to the pan. Bring back to a boil, cover, and simmer for about 20 minutes or until the meat and vegetables are just tender.

5 Skim away any remaining film that has risen to the top of the soup with a flat ladle. Blot the surface with absorbent paper towels to remove any fat. Adjust the seasoning according to taste.

6 Ladle the soup into warm bowls and sprinkle with freshly chopped parsley. Serve accompanied with fresh crusty bread.

VARIATION

This soup is just as delicious made with lean lamb or pork tenderloin. A vegetarian version can be made by omitting the beef and beef stock and using vegetable stock instead. Just before serving, stir in 6 ounces fresh bean curd, drained and diced. An even more substantial soup can be made by adding other root vegetables, such as rutabaga or turnip, instead of, or as well as, the carrot.

Mediterranean-style Fish Soup

Serves 4 • CALORIES PER SERVING: 270 • FAT CONTENT PER SERVING: 5.3 G

INGREDIENTS

1 tbsp olive oil
1 large onion, chopped
2 garlic cloves, finely chopped
1³/4 cups fresh fish stock
²/3 cup dry white wine
1 bay leaf
1 sprig each fresh thyme,
    rosemary, and oregano

1 pound firm white fish fillets
    (such as cod, monkfish or
    halibut), skinned and cut
    into 1-inch cubes
1 pound fresh mussels,
    prepared
14 ounce can chopped
    tomatoes
8 ounces peeled shrimp,
    thawed if frozen

salt and pepper
sprigs of thyme, to garnish

TO SERVE:
lemon wedges
4 slices toasted French bread,
    rubbed with cut garlic clove

1 Heat the oil in a pan and gently sauté the onion and garlic for 2–3 minutes, until softened.

2 Pour in the stock and wine and bring to a boil. Tie the bay leaf and herbs together with clean string and add to the saucepan, together with the fish and mussels. Stir well, cover, and simmer for 5 minutes.

3 Stir in the tomatoes and shrimp and continue to cook for a further 3–4 minutes, until piping hot and the fish is cooked through.

4 Discard the herbs and any mussels that have not opened. Season to taste, then ladle into warm bowls. Garnish with fresh thyme and serve with lemon wedges and toasted bread.

COOK'S TIP

Traditionally, the toasted bread is placed at the bottom of the bowl and the soup spooned over the top.
For convenience, use prepared, cooked shellfish mixtures, instead of fresh fish. Simply add to the soup with the tomatoes in step 3.

Tuscan Bean & Vegetable Soup

Serves 4 • Calories per serving: 156 • Fat content per serving: 1.5 g

INGREDIENTS

1 medium onion, chopped	5 cups fresh vegetable stock	TO SERVE:
1 garlic clove, finely chopped	1 tsp dried oregano	low-fat pesto sauce
2 celery stalks, sliced	15 ounce can mixed beans	(see page 146)
1 large carrot, diced	and legumes	crusty bread
14 ounce can chopped	2 medium zucchini, diced	
tomatoes	1 tbsp tomato paste	
$^2/_3$ cup Italian dry	salt and pepper	
red wine		

1 Place the prepared onion, garlic, celery, and carrot in a large saucepan. Stir in the tomatoes, red wine, vegetable stock, and oregano.

2 Bring the vegetable mixture to a boil, cover the pan, and simmer for about 15 minutes. Stir the beans and zucchini into the mixture, and continue to cook, uncovered, for a further 5 minutes.

3 Add the tomato paste and season well with salt and pepper to taste. Then heat through, stirring occasionally, for a further 2–3 minutes, but do not allow the mixture to boil again.

4 Ladle the soup into warm bowls and serve with a spoonful of low-fat pesto (see page 146) on each portion and accompanied with lots of fresh crusty bread.

VARIATION

For a more substantial soup, add 12 ounces diced lean cooked chicken or turkey with the tomato paste in step 3.

Lentil, Pasta, & Vegetable Soup

Serves 4 • CALORIES PER SERVING: 378 • FAT CONTENT PER SERVING: 4.9 G

INGREDIENTS

1 tbsp olive oil
1 medium onion, chopped
4 garlic cloves, finely chopped
12 ounces carrots, sliced
1 celery stalk, sliced
$1^{1}/_{4}$ cups red lentils

$2^{1}/_{2}$ cups fresh vegetable
   stock
3 cups boiling water
1 cup dried pasta
$2/_{3}$ cup natural low-fat
   unsweetened yogurt

salt and pepper
2 tbsp fresh parsley, chopped,
   to garnish

1 Heat the oil in a large saucepan and gently sauté the prepared onion, garlic, carrot, and celery, stirring gently, for about 5 minutes or until the vegetables begin to soften.

2 Add the lentils, stock, and boiling water. Season with salt and pepper to taste, stir, and bring back to a boil. Simmer, uncovered, for 15 minutes until the lentils are completely tender. Allow to cool for 10 minutes.

3 Meanwhile, bring another saucepan of water to a boil and cook the pasta according to the instructions on the packet. Drain well and set aside.

4 Place the soup in a blender and process until smooth. Return to a saucepan and add the pasta. Bring back to a simmer and heat for 2–3 minutes, until piping hot. Remove from the heat and stir in the yogurt. Adjust the seasoning if necessary.

5 Serve sprinkled with chopped parsley.

COOK'S TIP

Avoid boiling the soup once the yogurt has been added. Otherwise it will separate and become watery, spoiling the appearance of the soup.

Creamy Corn Soup

Serves 4 • CALORIES PER SERVING: 346 • FAT CONTENT PER SERVING: 2.4 G

INGREDIENTS

1 large onion, chopped	1 pound canned corn kernels	TO GARNISH:
1 large potato, peeled and	or frozen, drained or	3 1/2 ounces lean ham, diced
diced	thawed	2 tbsp snipped fresh chives
4 cups skim milk	1 tbsp cornstarch	
1 bay leaf	3 tbsp cold water	
1/2 tsp ground nutmeg	4 tbsp natural low-fat	
	unsweetened yogurt	
	salt and pepper	

1 Place the onion and potato in a large saucepan and pour in the milk. Add the bay leaf, nutmeg, and half the corn. Bring to a boil, cover, and simmer gently for 15 minutes, until the potato is softened. Stir the soup occasionally and keep the heat low so that the milk does not burn on the bottom of the pan.

2 Discard the bay leaf and leave the liquid to cool for 10 minutes. Transfer to a blender and process briefly. Alternatively, rub through a strainer.

3 Pour the smooth liquid into a saucepan. Blend the cornstarch with the cold water to make a paste and stir it into the soup.

4 Bring the soup back to a boil, stirring until it thickens, and add the remaining corn. Heat through for 2–3 minutes until piping hot.

5 Remove from the heat and season with salt and pepper. Stir in the yogurt. Ladle the soup into bowls, garnish, and serve.

VARIATION

For a more substantial soup, add 8 ounces flaked white crabmeat or peeled, cooked shrimp in step 4.

Tomato & Red Bell Pepper Soup

Serves 4 • CALORIES PER SERVING: 93 • FAT CONTENT PER SERVING: 1 G

INGREDIENTS

2 large red bell peppers
1 large onion, chopped
2 celery stalks, trimmed and
    chopped
1 garlic clove, crushed

2¹/₂ cups fresh vegetable
    stock
2 bay leaves
2 14-ounce cans plum
    tomatoes

salt and pepper
2 scallions, finely shredded,
    to garnish
crusty bread, to serve

1 Preheat the broiler. Halve and seed the bell peppers, arrange them on the broiler rack and cook, turning occasionally, for 8–10 minutes until softened and charred.

2 Leave to cool slightly, then carefully peel off the charred skin. Reserving a small piece for garnish, chop the bell pepper flesh and place in a large saucepan.

3 Mix in the onion, celery, and garlic. Add the stock and the bay leaves.

Bring to a boil, cover, and simmer for 15 minutes. Remove from the heat.

4 Stir in the tomatoes and transfer to a blender. Process for a few seconds until smooth. Return to the saucepan.

5 Season with salt and pepper to taste and heat for 3–4 minutes until piping hot. Ladle the soup into warm bowls and garnish with the reserved bell pepper cut into strips and the scallion. Serve with lots of fresh crusty bread.

COOK'S TIP

If you prefer a coarser, more robust soup, lightly mash the tomatoes with a wooden spoon and omit the blending process in step 4.

Carrot, Apple, & Celery Soup

Serves 4 • CALORIES PER SERVING: 150 • FAT CONTENT PER SERVING: 1.4 G

INGREDIENTS

2 pounds carrots, finely diced	3 medium-size eating	¼ large lemon
1 medium onion, chopped	apples	salt and pepper
3 celery stalks, trimmed and	2 tbsp tomato paste	celery leaves, washed and
diced	1 bay leaf	shredded, to garnish
4 cups fresh vegetable stock	2 tsp superfine sugar	

1 Place the prepared carrots, onion, and celery in a large saucepan and add the fresh vegetable stock. Bring to a boil, cover and simmer for about 10 minutes.

2 Meanwhile, peel, core, and dice 2 of the apples. Add the pieces of apple, tomato paste, bay leaf, and superfine sugar to the saucepan and bring to a boil. Reduce the heat, half cover the pan, and allow to simmer for 20 minutes. Remove and discard the bay leaf.

3 Meanwhile, wash, core, and cut the remaining apple into thin slices, leaving on the skin. Place the apple slices in a small saucepan and squeeze in the lemon juice. Heat gently and simmer for 1–2 minutes, until tender. Drain and set aside.

4 Place the carrot and apple mixture in a blender or food processor and blend until smooth. Alternatively, press the mixture through a strainer with the back of a wooden spoon, until smooth.

5 Gently reheat the soup if necessary and season with salt and pepper to taste. Ladle the soup into warm bowls and serve topped with the reserved apple slices and shredded celery leaves.

COOK'S TIP

Soaking light colored fruit in lemon juice prevents it from turning brown when exposed to the air.

Chilled Piquant Shrimp & Cucumber Soup

Serves 4 • CALORIES PER SERVING: 104 • FAT CONTENT PER SERVING: 1 G

INGREDIENTS

1 cucumber, peeled and diced
1²/3 cups fresh fish stock, chilled
²/3 cup tomato juice
1²/3 cup low-fat unsweetened yogurt

4¹/2 ounces peeled shrimp, thawed if frozen, roughly chopped
few drops Tabasco sauce
1 tbsp fresh mint, chopped
salt and white pepper
ice cubes, to serve

TO GARNISH:
sprigs of mint
cucumber slices
whole peeled shrimp

1 Place the diced cucumber in a blender or food processor and work for a few seconds until a smooth purée is formed. Alternatively, chop the cucumber finely and push through a strainer.

2 Transfer the cucumber to a bowl. Stir in the fish stock, tomato juice, yogurt, and shrimp, and mix well. Add the Tabasco sauce and season with salt and pepper to taste.

3 Stir in the chopped mint, cover, and chill in the refrigerator for at least 2 hours.

4 Ladle the soup into glass bowls and add a few ice cubes. Serve garnished with mint, cucumber slices, and whole shrimp.

VARIATION

Instead of shrimp, add white crabmeat or cooked ground chicken. For a vegetarian version of this soup, omit the shrimp and add an extra 4¹/2 ounces finely diced cucumber. Use fresh vegetable stock instead of fish stock.

Rosy Melon & Strawberries

Serves 4 • CALORIES PER SERVING: 83 • FAT CONTENT PER SERVING: 0.2 G

INGREDIENTS

1/4 honeydew melon	2/3 cup rosé wine	6 ounces small strawberries,
1/2 Charentais or Cantaloupe melon	2–3 tsp rosewater	washed and hulled
		rose petals, to garnish

1 Scoop out the seeds from both melons with a spoon. Then carefully remove the skin, taking care not to remove too much flesh.

2 Cut the melon flesh into thin strips and place in a bowl. Pour in the wine and sufficient rosewater to taste. Mix together gently, cover, and chill in the refrigerator for at least 2 hours.

3 Halve the strawberries and carefully mix into the melon. Allow the melon and strawberries to stand at room temperature for about 15 minutes for the flavors to develop fully.

4 Arrange the melon and strawberries on individual serving plates and serve sprinkled with a few rose petals.

COOK'S TIP

Rosewater is a distillation of rose petals. It is generally available from large pharmacies and leading supermarkets, as well as from more specialty food suppliers.

VARIATION

It does not matter whether the rosé wine is sweet or dry—although sweet wine contains more calories. Experiment with different types of melon. Varieties such as "Sweet Dream" have whitish-green flesh, while Charentais melons, which have orange flesh, are fragrant and go better with a dry wine. If you wish, soak the strawberries in the wine with the melon, but always allow the fruit to return to room temperature before serving.

Italian Platter

Serves 4 • CALORIES PER SERVING: 175 • FAT CONTENT PER SERVING: 7.6 G

INGREDIENTS

4¹/₂ ounces reduced-fat
  mozzarella cheese, drained
2 ounces lean prosciutto
14 ounce can artichoke
  hearts, drained
4 ripe figs
1 small mango

plain bread sticks,
  to serve

DRESSING:
1 small orange
1 tbsp sieved tomatoes
1 tsp wholegrain mustard

4 tbsp low-fat unsweetened
  yogurt
fresh basil leaves
salt and pepper

1 Cut the cheese into 12 sticks, 2½ inches long. Remove the fat from the prosciutto and slice the meat into 12 strips.

2 Carefully wrap a strip of prosciutto around each stick of cheese and arrange them neatly on a serving platter.

3 Halve the artichoke hearts and cut the figs into quarters. Arrange them on the serving platter in groups.

4 Peel the mango, then slice it down each side of the large, flat central pit. Slice the flesh into strips and arrange them so that they form a fan shape on the serving platter.

5 To make the dressing, pare the rind from half of the orange using a vegetable peeler. Cut the rind into small strips and place them in a bowl. Extract the juice from the orange and add it to the bowl containing the rind.

6 Add the sieved tomatoes, mustard, yogurt, and seasoning to the bowl and mix together. Shred the basil leaves and mix them into the dressing.

7 Spoon the dressing into a small dish and serve with the Italian Platter, accompanied with bread sticks.

Breakfast Muffins

Serves 4 • CALORIES PER SERVING: 270 • FAT CONTENT PER SERVING: 12.3 G

INGREDIENTS

2 whole wheat English muffins	4 medium eggs	4 tbsp fresh vegetable stock
8 slices lean bacon	2 large tomatoes	salt and pepper
	2 large flat mushrooms	1 small bunch fresh chives, snipped, to garnish

1 Preheat the broiler. Cut the muffins in half and toast them for 1–2 minutes on the open side. Set aside and keep warm.

2 Trim off all visible fat from the bacon and broil for 2–3 minutes on each side. Drain on absorbent paper towels and keep warm.

3 Place 4 egg-poaching rings in a skillet and pour in enough water to cover the base of the pan. Bring to a boil and reduce the heat to a simmer. Carefully break one egg into each ring and poach gently for 5–6 minutes until set.

4 Meanwhile, cut the tomatoes into 8 thick slices and arrange on a piece of kitchen foil on the broiler rack. Broil for 2–3 minutes, until just cooked. Season to taste.

5 Peel and thickly slice the mushrooms. Place in a pan with the stock, bring to a boil, cover, and simmer for 4–5 minutes until cooked. Drain thoroughly, set aside, and keep warm.

6 To serve, arrange the tomato and mushroom slices on the toasted muffins and top each with 2 slices of bacon. Arrange an egg on top of each and sprinkle with pepper. Garnish with snipped chives and serve.

VARIATION

Omit the bacon for a vegetarian version and use more tomatoes and mushrooms instead. Alternatively, include a broiled low-fat bean curd or soy protein burger.

Cheesy Ham & Celery Savory

Serves 4 • CALORIES PER SERVING: 155 • FAT CONTENT PER SERVING: 6.9 G

INGREDIENTS

4 celery stalks
12 thin slices of lean ham
1 bunch scallions
6 ounces low-fat soft cheese
    with garlic and herbs

6 tbsp low-fat unsweetened
    yogurt
4 tbsp Parmesan cheese,
    freshly grated
celery salt and pepper

TO SERVE:
tomato salad
crusty bread

1 Wash the celery, remove the leaves, and slice the celery stalks into 3 equal portions.

2 Cut any visible fat off the ham and lay the slices on a chopping board. Place a piece of celery on each piece of ham and roll up. Place 3 ham and celery rolls in each of 4 small, heatproof dishes.

3 Trim the scallions, then finely shred both the white and green parts. Sprinkle the shredded scallions over the ham and celery rolls and season with celery salt and pepper.

4 Mix together the soft cheese and yogurt and spoon over the ham and celery rolls.

5 Preheat the broiler. Sprinkle each portion with 1 tbsp grated Parmesan cheese and broil for 6–7 minutes until hot and the cheese has formed a crust. If the cheese starts to brown too quickly, lower the broiler setting slightly.

6 Serve with a tomato salad and lots of fresh crusty bread.

COOK'S TIP

Parmesan is useful in low-fat recipes because its intense flavor means you need to use only a small amount.

Parsleyed Chicken & Ham Pâté

Serves 4 • CALORIES PER SERVING: 132 • FAT CONTENT PER SERVING: 1.8 G

INGREDIENTS

8 ounces lean, skinless chicken, cooked	2 tbsp lime juice	TO SERVE:
3¹/₂ ounces lean ham, trimmed	1 garlic clove, peeled	wedges of lime
small bunch fresh parsley	¹/₂ cup low-fat unsweetened yogurt	crispbread
1 tsp lime rind, grated	salt and pepper	
	1 tsp lime zest, to garnish	

1 Dice the chicken and ham and place in a blender or food processor. Add the parsley, lime rind and juice, and garlic and process well until finely ground. Alternatively, finely chop the chicken, ham, parsley, and garlic and place in a mixing bowl. Mix gently with the lime rind and juice.

2 Transfer the mixture to a bowl and mix in the yogurt. Season with salt and pepper to taste, cover, and set aside to chill in the refrigerator for about 30 minutes.

3 Transfer the pâté into individual serving dishes and garnish with lime zest. Serve the pâtés with lime wedges and crispbread.

VARIATION

This pâté can be made equally successfully with other kinds of ground, lean, cooked meat, such as turkey, beef, and pork. Alternatively, replace the chicken and ham with peeled shrimp and/or white crabmeat or with canned tuna in water, drained. Remember that removing the skin from poultry reduces the fat content of any dish.

Spinach Cheese Molds

Serves 4 • CALORIES PER SERVING: 64 • FAT CONTENT PER SERVING: 0.2 G

INGREDIENTS

3 1/2 ounces fresh spinach
leaves
10 1/2 ounces skim milk soft
cheese
2 garlic cloves, crushed

sprigs of fresh parsley,
tarragon, and chives, finely
chopped
salt and pepper

TO SERVE:
salad greens and fresh herbs
pita bread

1 Trim the stalks from the spinach leaves. Rinse the leaves under running water. Pack the leaves into a saucepan while still wet, cover, and cook for 3–4 minutes until wilted—they will cook in the steam from the wet leaves (do not overcook). Drain well and pat dry with absorbent paper towels.

2 Base-line 4 small pudding basins or individual ramekin dishes with baking parchment. Line the basins or ramekins with spinach leaves so that

the leaves overhang the edges if they are large enough to do so.

3 Place the cheese in a bowl and add the garlic and herbs. Mix together thoroughly and season to taste.

4 Spoon the cheese and herb mixture into the basins or ramekins and pull over the overlapping spinach to cover the cheese, or lay extra leaves to cover the top. Place a baking paper round on top of each dish and weigh down with

a 4 ounce weight. Chill in the refrigerator for 1 hour.

5 Remove the weights and peel off the paper. Loosen the molds by running a small spatula around the edges of each dish and turn them out onto individual plates.

6 Serve with a mixture of salad greens and fresh herbs, and warm pita bread.

Soufflé Omelet

Serves 4 • CALORIES PER SERVING: 141 • FAT CONTENT PER SERVING: 9.7 G

INGREDIENTS

6 ounces cherry tomatoes	small bunch fresh thyme	salt and pepper
8 ounces mixed mushrooms	4 medium eggs, separated	fresh thyme sprigs, to garnish
(such as button, chestnut,	4 medium egg whites	
shiitake, oyster)	4 tsp olive oil	
4 tbsp fresh vegetable stock	1 ounce arugula leaves	

1 Halve the tomatoes and place them in a saucepan. Wipe the mushrooms with paper towels, trim if necessary, and slice if large. Place in the saucepan.

2 Add the stock and thyme to the pan. Bring to a boil, cover, and simmer for 5–6 minutes until tender. Drain, remove the thyme and discard, and keep the mixture warm.

3 Meanwhile, whisk the egg yolks with 8 tablespoons of water until frothy. In a clean, greasefree bowl, mix the 8 egg whites until stiff and dry.

4 Spoon the egg yolk mixture into the egg whites and, using a metal spoon, fold the whites and yolks into each other until well mixed. Do not knock out too much of the air.

5 For each omelet, brush a small omelet pan with 1 tsp oil and heat until hot. Pour in a quarter of the egg mixture and cook for 4–5 minutes, until the mixture has set.

6 Preheat the broiler and finish cooking the omelet for 2–3 minutes.

7 Transfer the omelet to a warm serving plate. Fill the omelet with a few arugula leaves, and a quarter of the mushroom and tomato mixture. Flip over the top of the omelet, garnish with sprigs of thyme, and serve.

Broiled Rice & Tuna Bell Peppers

Serves 4 • CALORIES PER SERVING: 383 • FAT CONTENT PER SERVING: 6.8 G

INGREDIENTS

1/3 cup wild rice	11 1/2 ounce can corn kernels	2 tbsp dry white bread crumbs
1/3 cup brown rice	(with no added sugar or	1 tbsp Parmesan cheese,
4 assorted medium bell	salt), drained	freshly grated
peppers	3 1/2 ounces reduced-fat	salt and pepper
7 ounce can tuna fish in	Cheddar cheese, grated	fresh basil leaves, to garnish
water, drained and flaked	1 bunch fresh basil leaves,	crisp salad leaves, to serve
	shredded	

1 Place the wild rice and brown rice in two different saucepans, cover with water, and cook according to the instructions on the packet. Drain well.

2 Meanwhile, preheat the broiler. Halve the bell peppers, remove the seeds and stalks, and arrange the bell peppers on the broiler rack, cut side down. Cook for 5 minutes, turn over, and cook for 4–5 minutes.

3 Transfer the cooked rice to a mixing bowl and add the flaked tuna and drained corn. Gently fold in the grated Cheddar. Mix in the basil leaves and season to taste.

4 Divide the tuna and rice mixture into 8 equal portions. Pile each portion into each cooked bell pepper half. Mix together the bread crumbs and Parmesan cheese and sprinkle the mixture over each bell pepper.

5 Place the bell peppers back under the broiler for 4–5 minutes, until hot and golden-brown. Serve immediately, garnished with fresh basil leaves and accompanied with fresh, crisp salad leaves.

Baked Potatoes with a Spicy Filling

Serves 4 • CALORIES PER SERVING: 354 • FAT CONTENT PER SERVING: 5.9 G

INGREDIENTS

4 baking potatoes, each about
  10$^{1}/_{2}$ ounces
1 tbsp vegetable oil (optional)
14 ounce can garbanzo
  beans, drained

1 tsp ground coriander
1 tsp ground cumin
4 tbsp fresh cilantro, chopped
$^{2}/_{3}$ cup low-fat unsweetened
  yogurt

salt and pepper
salad, to serve

1 Preheat the oven to 400°F. Scrub the potatoes and pat them dry on absorbent paper towels. Prick them all over with a fork, brush with oil (if using), and season to taste with salt and pepper.

2 Place the potatoes on a cookie sheet and bake for 1–1¼ hours, or until cooked through. Cool for 10 minutes.

3 Meanwhile, mash the garbanzo beans with a fork or potato masher. Stir in the spices and half the

chopped cilantro. Cover and set aside.

4 Halve the cooked potatoes and scoop the flesh into a bowl, keeping the shells intact. Mash the flesh until smooth and gently mix into the garbanzo bean mixture with the yogurt. Season well with salt and pepper.

5 Fill the potato shells with the potato and garbanzo bean mixture and place on a cookie sheet. Return the potatoes to the oven and bake for

10–15 minutes, until heated through.

6 Serve sprinkled with the remaining chopped cilantro and a fresh salad.

COOK'S TIP

For an even lower fat version of this recipe, bake the potatoes without oiling them first.

Spinach Crêpes with Curried Crab

Serves 4 • CALORIES PER SERVING: 259 • FAT CONTENT PER SERVING: 5.9 G

INGREDIENTS

4 ounces buckwheat flour
1 large egg, beaten
1¼ cups skim milk
4½ ounces frozen spinach,
    thawed, well-drained, and
    chopped
2 tsp vegetable oil

FILLING:
12 ounces white crabmeat
1 tsp mild curry powder
1 tbsp mango chutney
1 tbsp reduced-calorie
    mayonnaise
2 tbsp low-fat unsweetened
    yogurt

2 tbsp fresh cilantro, chopped

TO SERVE:
salad greens
lemon wedges

1 Sift the flour into a bowl and remove any husks that remain in the strainer.

2 Make a well in the center of the flour and add the egg. Gradually whisk in the milk, then blend in the spinach. Transfer the batter to a pitcher and allow to stand for 30 minutes.

3 To make the filling, mix together all the ingredients, except the cilantro, in a bowl, cover, and chill until required.

4 Whisk the batter. Brush a crêpe pan with a little oil, heat until hot, and pour in enough batter to cover the base thinly. Cook for 1–2 minutes until set, turn over, and cook for 1 minute until golden. Transfer to a warmed plate. Repeat to make 8 pancakes, layering them on the plate with baking parchment.

5 Stir the cilantro into the crab mixture. Fold each pancake into quarters. Open one fold and fill with the crab mixture. Serve warm, with salad greens and lemon wedges.

VARIATION

Try lean diced chicken in a light white sauce or peeled shrimp instead of the crab.

Meat & Poultry

The increased interest in healthy eating means
that most supermarkets and butchers now offer
special cuts of lean meat. Although they are often
slightly more expensive than standard cuts, it is
worth buying this meat and spending a little extra
time cooking it carefully to enhance the flavor.
You will not need to buy as much if you
combine the meat with thoughtfully
chosen and prepared vegetables.

Look for packs of low- or reduced-fat ground meat
in your local supermarket, and include it in burgers
or serve it in a flavor-filled sauce with rice or your
favorite pasta.

Cut any visible fat from beef and pork before
you cook it. Chicken and turkey are lower in fat
than red meats, and you can make them even
healthier by removing the skin. Duck is a rich meat
with a distinctive flavor, and you need only a small
amount to create apparently extravagant,
flavorful dishes that are healthy, too.

Pan-cooked Pork with Fennel & Aniseed

Serves 4 • CALORIES PER SERVING: 242 • FAT CONTENT PER SERVING: 6.4 G

INGREDIENTS

4 lean pork chops,
    4¹/2 ounces each
¹/3 cup brown rice, cooked
1 tsp orange rind, grated
4 scallions, trimmed and
    finely chopped
¹/2 tsp aniseed

1 tbsp olive oil
1 fennel bulb, trimmed and
    thinly sliced
2 cups unsweetened orange
    juice
1 tbsp cornstarch
2 tbsp Pernod

salt and pepper
fennel fronds, to garnish
cooked vegetables, to serve

1 Trim away any excess fat from the pork chops. Using a small, sharp knife, make a slit in the center of each chop to create a pocket.

2 Mix the cooked rice, orange rind, scallions, salt and pepper to taste, and aniseed together in a bowl. Press the mixture into the pocket of each pork chop, then press gently to seal together.

3 Heat the oil in a skillet and fry the pork chops on each side for 2–3 minutes, until golden.

4 Add the sliced fennel and orange juice to the skillet, bring to a boil, and simmer for 15–20 minutes or until the meat is tender and cooked through. Remove the pork and fennel with a slotted spoon and transfer to a warm serving plate.

5 Blend the cornstarch and Pernod together in a small bowl. Add the cornstarch mixture to the pan and stir into the pan juices. Cook for 2–3 minutes, stirring, until the sauce thickens.

6 Pour the Pernod sauce over the pork chops, garnish with fennel fronds, and serve with a selection of cooked vegetables, if you wish.

Pork Stroganoff

Serves 4 • Calories per serving: 197 • Fat content per serving: 7 g

INGREDIENTS

12 ounces lean pork tenderloin
1 tbsp vegetable oil
1 medium onion, chopped
2 garlic cloves, crushed
1 ounce all-purpose flour
2 tbsp tomato paste
1³/₄ cups fresh chicken or
    vegetable stock

4¹/₂ ounces button
    mushrooms, sliced
1 large green bell pepper,
    seeded and diced
¹/₂ tsp ground nutmeg
4 tbsp low-fat unsweetened
    yogurt, plus extra to serve
salt and pepper

white rice, freshly boiled,
    to serve

TO GARNISH:
chopped fresh parsley
ground nutmeg

1 Using a sharp knife, trim away any excess fat and silver skin from the pork, then cut the meat into slices ¹/₂ inch thick.

2 Heat the oil in a large skillet and gently fry the pork, onion, and garlic for 4–5 minutes until lightly browned.

3 Stir in the flour and tomato paste, pour in the stock, and stir to mix thoroughly.

4 Add the mushrooms, bell pepper, seasoning, and nutmeg. Bring to a boil, cover, and simmer for 20 minutes, until the pork is tender and cooked through.

5 Remove the saucepan from the heat and stir in the yogurt.

6 Serve the pork and sauce on a bed of rice, garnished with chopped parsley. Spoon the extra yogurt on top of the pork

and mushrooms and dust with ground nutmeg.

COOK'S TIP

You can buy ready-made meat, vegetable, and fish stocks from leading supermarkets. Although more expensive, they are better nutritionally than stock cubes, which are high in salt and artificial flavorings. Homemade stock is best of all.

Pan-cooked Pork Medallions with Apples & Cider

Serves 4 • CALORIES PER SERVING: 192 • FAT CONTENT PER SERVING: 5.7 G

INGREDIENTS

8 lean pork medallions, about
   1³/₄ ounces each
2 tsp vegetable oil
1 medium onion, finely sliced
1 tsp superfine sugar
1 tsp dried sage

²/₃ cup hard cider
²/₃ cup fresh chicken or
   vegetable stock
1 green-skinned apple
1 red-skinned apple
1 tbsp lemon juice

salt and pepper
fresh sage leaves, to garnish
freshly cooked vegetables,
   to serve

1 Discard the string from the pork and trim away any excess fat. Re-tie with clean string and set aside until required.

2 Heat the oil in a skillet and gently sauté the onion for 5 minutes, until softened. Add the sugar and cook for 3–4 minutes until golden.

3 Add the pork to the pan and cook for 2 minutes on each side, until browned. Add the sage, cider, and stock. Bring to a boil and then simmer for 20 minutes.

4 Meanwhile, core and cut each apple into 8 wedges. Toss the apple wedges in lemon juice so that they do not discolor and turn brown.

5 Add the apples to the pork and mix gently. Season and cook for 3–4 minutes, until tender.

6 Remove the string from the pork and serve immediately, garnished with fresh sage and accompanied with freshly cooked vegetables.

COOK'S TIP

If pork medallions are not available, buy 14 ounces pork tenderloin and slice it into evenly-sized medallions yourself.

Red Roast Pork with Bell Peppers

Serves 4 • CALORIES PER SERVING: 282 • FAT CONTENT PER SERVING: 5 G

INGREDIENTS

1 pound lean pork tenderloin
6 tbsp dark soy sauce
2 tbsp dry sherry
1 tsp five-spice powder
2 garlic cloves, crushed
1-inch piece fresh ginger root, finely chopped

1 large red bell pepper
1 large yellow bell pepper
1 large orange bell pepper
4 tbsp superfine sugar
2 tbsp red wine vinegar

TO GARNISH:
scallions, shredded
fresh chives, snipped

1 Trim away any excess fat and silver skin from the pork and place in a shallow dish.

2 Mix together the soy sauce, sherry, five-spice powder, garlic, and ginger. Spoon over the pork, cover, and marinate in the refrigerator for at least 1 hour.

3 Preheat the oven to 375°F. Drain the pork, reserving the marinade. Place the pork on a roasting rack over a roasting pan. Cook in the oven, occasionally basting with the marinade, for 1 hour or until cooked through.

4 Meanwhile, halve and seed the bell peppers. Cut each bell pepper half into 3 equal portions. Arrange them on a cookie sheet and bake alongside the pork for the last 30 minutes of cooking time.

5 Place the superfine sugar and vinegar in a small saucepan and heat gently over a low heat until the sugar has completely dissolved. Bring to a boil and simmer for 3–4 minutes, until syrupy.

6 As soon as the pork is cooked, remove from the oven and brush with the sugar syrup. Allow to stand for 5 minutes, then slice, and arrange on a warm platter with the bell peppers. Garnish and serve.

Pork with Ratatouille Sauce

Serves 4 • CALORIES PER SERVING: 214 • FAT CONTENT PER SERVING: 5.6 G

INGREDIENTS

4 lean, boneless pork chops,
about 4¹/2 ounces each
1 tsp dried mixed herbs
salt and pepper
baked potatoes, to serve

SAUCE:
1 medium onion
1 garlic clove
1 small green bell pepper
1 small yellow bell pepper
1 medium zucchini

3¹/2 ounces button
mushrooms
14 ounce can chopped
tomatoes
2 tbsp tomato paste
1 tsp dried mixed herbs
1 tsp superfine sugar

1 To make the sauce, peel and chop the onion and garlic. Seed and dice the bell peppers. Trim and dice the zucchini. Wipe and halve the mushrooms.

2 Place all of the vegetables in a saucepan and stir in the chopped tomatoes and tomato paste. Add the dried herbs, sugar, and plenty of seasoning. Bring to a boil, cover, and simmer for 20 minutes.

3 Meanwhile, preheat the broiler. Trim away any excess fat from the chops, then season on both sides, and rub in the dried mixed herbs. Cook the chops for 5 minutes, then turn over, and cook for a further 6–7 minutes until cooked through.

4 Drain the pork chops on absorbent paper towels and serve accompanied with the sauce and baked potatoes, if wished.

COOK'S TIP

This vegetable sauce could be served with any other broiled or baked meat or fish. It would also make an excellent alternative filling for the Spinach Crêpes on page 46.

Beef & Orange Curry

Serves 4 • CALORIES PER SERVING: 283 • FAT CONTENT PER SERVING: 10.5 G

INGREDIENTS

1 tbsp vegetable oil
8 ounces shallots, halved
2 garlic cloves, crushed
1 pound lean rump or sirloin
   beef, trimmed and cut
   into $^3/_4$ inch cubes
3 tbsp curry paste
2 cups fresh beef stock
4 medium oranges

2 tsp cornstarch
salt and pepper
2 tbsp fresh cilantro, chopped,
   to garnish
Basmati rice, freshly boiled,
   to serve

RAITA:
$^1/_2$ cucumber, finely diced
3 tbsp fresh mint, chopped
$^2/_3$ cup low-fat unsweetened
   yogurt

1 Heat the oil in a large saucepan. Gently fry the shallots, garlic, and the cubes of beef for 5 minutes, stirring occasionally, until the beef is evenly browned all over.

2 Blend together the curry paste and stock. Add the mixture to the beef and stir to mix. Bring to a boil, cover, and simmer for 1 hour, or until the meat is tender.

3 Grate the rind of one orange. Extract the juice from the orange and from a second orange. Peel the two remaining oranges, removing as much pith as possible. Slice between each segment and remove the flesh.

4 Blend the cornstarch with the orange juice. At the end of the cooking time, stir the orange rind into the beef, along with

the orange and cornstarch mixture. Bring to a boil and simmer, stirring, for 3–4 minutes, until the sauce thickens. Season and stir in the orange segments.

5 To make the raita, mix the cucumber with the mint, and stir in the yogurt. Season to taste.

6 Garnish the curry and serve with rice and the cucumber raita.

Pan-seared Beef with Ginger, Pineapple, & Chili

Serves 4 • CALORIES PER SERVING: 191 • FAT CONTENT PER SERVING: 5.1 G

INGREDIENTS

4 lean beef steaks (such as rump, sirloin, or fillet), 3½ ounces each
2 tbsp ginger wine
1-inch piece fresh ginger root, finely chopped
1 garlic clove, crushed
1 tsp ground chili
1 tsp vegetable oil

salt and pepper
red chili strips, to garnish

TO SERVE:
freshly cooked noodles
2 scallions, shredded

RELISH:
8 ounces fresh pineapple
1 small red bell pepper
1 red chili
2 tbsp light soy sauce
1 piece preserved ginger in syrup, drained and chopped

1 Trim any excess fat from the beef. Using a meat mallet or covered rolling pin, pound the steaks until ½ inch thick. Season on both sides and place in a shallow dish.

2 Mix the ginger wine, ginger root, garlic, and chili and pour over the meat. Cover and chill for 30 minutes.

3 Meanwhile, make the relish. Peel and finely chop the pineapple and place it in a bowl. Halve, seed, and finely chop the bell pepper and chili. Stir into the pineapple, together with the soy sauce and preserved ginger. Cover and chill until required.

4 Brush a ridged skillet with the oil and heat until very hot. Drain the beef and add to the pan, pressing down to seal. Lower the heat and cook for 5 minutes. Turn the steaks over and cook for 5 minutes.

5 Drain the steaks on paper towels and transfer to serving plates. Garnish with chili strips, and serve with noodles, scallions, and the relish.

Beef & Tomato Gratin

Serves 4 • Calories per serving: 319 • Fat content per serving: 10.3 g

INGREDIENTS

12 ounces lean ground beef
1 large onion, finely chopped
1 tsp dried mixed herbs
1 tbsp all-purpose flour
1 1/4 cups beef stock
1 tbsp tomato paste
2 large tomatoes, thinly sliced
4 medium zucchini, thinly sliced

2 tbsp cornstarch
1 1/4 cups skim milk
2/3 cup low-fat unsweetened yogurt
1 medium egg yolk
4 tbsp Parmesan cheese, freshly grated
salt and pepper

TO SERVE:
crusty bread
steamed vegetables

1 Preheat the oven to 375°F. In a large pan, dry-fry the beef and onion for 4–5 minutes until browned.

2 Stir in the herbs, flour, stock, and tomato paste, and season. Bring to a boil and simmer for 30 minutes until thickened.

3 Transfer the beef mixture to an ovenproof gratin dish.

Cover with a layer of the sliced tomatoes and then add a layer of sliced zucchini. Set aside until required.

4 Blend the cornstarch with a little milk in a small bowl. Pour the remaining milk into a saucepan and bring to a boil. Add the cornstarch mixture and cook, stirring, for 1–2 minutes, until thickened. Remove from

the heat and beat in the yogurt and egg yolk. Season with salt and pepper to taste.

5 Place the dish on a cookie sheet. Spread the white sauce over the layer of zucchini and sprinkle with grated Parmesan. Bake in the oven for 25–30 minutes, until golden brown. Serve with lots of fresh crusty bread and steamed vegetables.

Sweet & Sour Venison Stir-fry

Serves 4 • CALORIES PER SERVING: 174 • FAT CONTENT PER SERVING: 1.9 G

INGREDIENTS

1 bunch scallions	1-inch piece fresh ginger root,	8 ounce can pineapple pieces
1 red bell pepper	finely chopped	in natural juice, drained
3¹/₂ ounces snow peas	3 tbsp light soy sauce, plus	1 ounce bean sprouts
3¹/₂ ounces baby corn cobs	extra for serving	freshly cooked rice, to serve
12 ounces lean venison steak	1 tbsp white wine vinegar	
1 tbsp vegetable oil	2 tbsp dry sherry	
1 clove garlic, crushed	2 tsp clear honey	

1 Trim the scallions and cut into 1-inch pieces. Halve and seed the bell pepper and cut it into 1-inch pieces. Top and tail the snow peas and trim the baby corn cobs.

2 Using a sharp knife, trim the excess fat from the meat and cut it into thin strips. Heat the oil in a large skillet or preheated wok until hot and stir-fry the meat, garlic, and ginger for 5 minutes.

3 Add the prepared scallion, bell pepper, snow peas, and baby corn cobs to the pan, then add the soy sauce, vinegar, sherry, and honey. Stir-fry for a further 5 minutes, keeping the heat high.

4 Carefully stir in the pineapple pieces and bean sprouts and cook for a further 1–2 minutes to heat through. Serve with freshly cooked rice and extra soy sauce for dipping.

VARIATION

For a quick and nutritious meal-in-one, cook 8 ounces egg noodles in boiling water for 3–4 minutes. Drain well and add to the pan in step 4, together with the pineapple and bean sprouts. Stir well to mix. You will have to add an extra 2 tbsp soy sauce with the pineapple and bean sprouts so that the stir-fry does not dry out.

Venison & Garlic Mash

Serves 4 • CALORIES PER SERVING: 503 • FAT CONTENT PER SERVING: 6.1 G

INGREDIENTS

8 medallions of venison,
  2$^3/_4$ ounces each
1 tbsp vegetable oil
1 red onion, chopped
$^2/_3$ cup fresh beef stock
$^2/_3$ cup red wine
3 tbsp redcurrant jelly

3$^1/_2$ ounces dried, pitted
  prunes
2 tsp cornstarch
2 tbsp brandy
salt and pepper

GARLIC MASH:
2 pounds potatoes, peeled and
  diced
$^1/_2$ tsp garlic paste
2 tbsp low-fat unsweetened
  yogurt
4 tbsp fresh parsley, chopped

1 Trim off any excess fat from the meat and season with salt and pepper on both sides.

2 Heat the oil in a pan and fry the medallions with the onions on a high heat for 2 minutes on each side until browned all over.

3 Lower the heat and pour in the stock and wine. Add the redcurrant jelly and prunes and stir until the jelly melts. Bring to a boil, cover, and simmer for 10 minutes until cooked through.

4 To make the garlic mash, place the potatoes in a pan and add enough water to cover. Bring to a boil and cook for 8–10 minutes, until tender. Drain.

5 Mash the potatoes. Add the garlic paste, yogurt, and parsley and blend thoroughly. Season, set aside, and keep warm.

6 Remove the medallions from the skillet with a slotted spoon and keep warm.

7 Blend the cornstarch with the brandy in a small bowl and add to the pan juices. Heat, stirring, until thickened. Season with salt and pepper to taste.

8 Transfer the venison to serving plates and serve with the redcurrant and prune sauce and garlic mash.

Venison Meatballs with Sherried Kumquat Sauce

Serves 4 • CALORIES PER SERVING: 178 • FAT CONTENT PER SERVING: 2.1 G

INGREDIENTS

1 pound lean ground venison
1 small leek, finely chopped
1 medium carrot, finely grated
1/2 tsp ground nutmeg
1 medium egg white, lightly
  beaten
salt and pepper

TO SERVE:
freshly cooked pasta or
  noodles
freshly cooked vegetables

SAUCE:
3 1/2 ounces kumquats
1/2 ounce superfine sugar
2/3 cup water
4 tbsp dry sherry
1 tsp cornstarch

1 Place the venison in a mixing bowl, together with the leek, carrot, seasoning, and nutmeg. Add the egg white and bind the ingredients together with your hands until the mixture is well molded and firm.

2 Divide the mixture into 16 equal portions. Using your fingers, form each portion into a small, round ball.

3 Bring a large saucepan of water to a boil. Arrange the meatballs on a layer of baking parchment in a steamer or large strainer and place over the boiling water. Cover and steam for 10 minutes, until cooked through.

4 Meanwhile, make the sauce. Wash and thinly slice the kumquats. Place them in a saucepan with the sugar and water and

bring to a boil. Simmer for 2–3 minutes until tender.

5 Blend the sherry and cornstarch together and add to the pan. Heat through, stirring, until the sauce thickens. Season.

6 Drain the meatballs and transfer to a serving plate. Spoon the sauce on top and serve with pasta and vegetables, if wished.

Fruity Lamb Casserole

Serves 4 • CALORIES PER SERVING: 280 • FAT CONTENT PER SERVING: 11.6 G

INGREDIENTS

1 pound lean lamb, trimmed
   and cut into 1-inch cubes
1 tsp ground cinnamon
1 tsp ground coriander
1 tsp ground cumin
2 tsp olive oil
1 medium red onion, finely
   chopped

1 garlic clove, crushed
14 ounce can chopped
   tomatoes
2 tbsp tomato paste
4^1/$_2$ ounces dried apricots
1 tsp superfine sugar
1^1/$_4$ cups vegetable stock
salt and pepper

1 small bunch fresh cilantro,
   to garnish
brown rice, steamed couscous,
   or bulgar wheat, to serve

---

1 Preheat the oven to 350°F. Place the meat in a bowl and add the cinnamon, coriander, cumin, and oil. Mix so that the lamb is well coated in the spices.

2 Heat a nonstick skillet for a few seconds until it is hot, then add the spiced lamb. Reduce the heat and cook for 4–5 minutes, stirring, until browned all over. Using a slotted spoon, remove the lamb and transfer to a large casserole.

3 In the same skillet, cook the onion, garlic, tomatoes, and tomato paste for 5 minutes. Season to taste. Stir in the apricots and sugar, add the stock, and bring to a boil.

4 Spoon the sauce over the lamb and mix well. Cover and cook in the oven for 1 hour, removing the lid for the last 10 minutes.

5 Roughly chop the cilantro and sprinkle over the casserole to garnish. Serve with boiled brown rice, steamed couscous, or bulgar wheat.

Lamb, Bell Pepper, & Couscous

Serves 4 • CALORIES PER SERVING: 522 • FAT CONTENT PER SERVING: 12.5 G

INGREDIENTS

2 medium red onions, sliced
juice of 1 lemon
1 large red bell pepper, seeded
    and thickly sliced
1 large green bell pepper,
    seeded and thickly sliced
1 large orange bell pepper,
    seeded and thickly sliced
pinch of saffron strands

cinnamon stick, broken
1 tbsp clear honey
1¼ cups vegetable stock
2 tsp olive oil
12 ounces lean lamb fillet,
    trimmed and sliced
1 tsp harissa paste
7 ounce can chopped
    tomatoes

15 ounce can garbanzo
    beans, drained
12 ounces couscous
2 tsp ground cinnamon
salt and pepper

1 Toss the red onions in the lemon juice and put in a pan. Add the bell peppers, saffron, cinnamon stick, and honey. Pour in the vegetable stock, bring to a boil, cover, and leave to simmer for 5 minutes.

2 Meanwhile, heat the olive oil in a skillet and gently fry the lamb for 3–4 minutes, until it is well browned all over.

3 Using a slotted spoon, drain the lamb and transfer it to the pan with the onions and peppers. Season and stir in the harissa paste, tomatoes, and garbanzo beans. Mix well, bring back to a boil, and simmer, uncovered, for 20 minutes.

4 Meanwhile, soak the couscous, following the instructions on the packet. Bring a saucepan of water to a boil. Transfer the couscous to a steamer or strainer lined with cheesecloth and place over the pan of boiling water. Cover and steam as directed.

5 Transfer the couscous to a warm serving platter and dust with ground cinnamon. Discard the cinnamon stick and serve the stew with the couscous.

Hot Pot Chops

Serves 4 • CALORIES PER SERVING: 252 • FAT CONTENT PER SERVING: 11.3 G

INGREDIENTS

4 lean, boned lamb leg steaks,
    about 4¹/₂ ounces each
1 small onion, thinly sliced
1 medium carrot, thinly sliced
1 medium potato, thinly sliced

1 tsp olive oil
1 tsp dried rosemary
salt and pepper
fresh rosemary, to garnish

freshly steamed green
    vegetables, to serve

1 Preheat the oven to 350°F. Using a sharp knife, trim any excess fat from the lamb steaks.

2 Season both sides of the steaks well with salt and pepper and arrange them on a cookie sheet or ovenproof dish.

3 Alternate layers of sliced onion, carrot, and potato on top of each lamb steak.

4 Brush the tops of the potato lightly with oil, season well with salt and pepper to taste, and then sprinkle with a little dried rosemary.

5 Bake the hot pot chops in the oven for about 25–30 minutes, until the lamb is tender and cooked through.

6 Drain the lamb on absorbent paper towels and transfer to a warmed serving plate.

7 Garnish with fresh rosemary and serve with a selection of green vegetables.

VARIATION

This recipe would work equally well with boneless chicken breasts. Pound the chicken slightly with a meat mallet or covered rolling pin so that the pieces are the same thickness throughout.

Minty Lamb Burgers

Serves 4 • CALORIES PER SERVING: 237 • FAT CONTENT PER SERVING: 7.8 G

INGREDIENTS

12 ounces lean lamb, ground
1 medium onion, finely
    chopped
4 tbsp dry whole wheat
    bread crumbs
2 tbsp mint jelly
salt and pepper

TO SERVE:
4 whole wheat rolls, split
4 large tomatoes, sliced
small piece of cucumber, sliced
lettuce leaves

RELISH:
4 tbsp low-fat unsweetened
    yogurt
1 tbsp mint jelly, softened
2-inch piece of cucumber,
    finely diced
1 tbsp fresh mint, chopped

1 Place the lamb in a large bowl and mix in the onion, bread crumbs, and jelly. Season well, then mold the ingredients together with your hands to form a firm mixture.

2 Divide the mixture into 4 and shape each portion into a round measuring 4 inches across. Place the rounds on a plate lined with baking parchment and leave to chill for 30 minutes.

3 Preheat the broiler. Line a broiler rack with baking parchment, securing the ends under the rack, and place the burgers on top. Cook for 8 minutes, then turn over the burgers, and cook for a further 7 minutes, or until completely cooked through.

4 Meanwhile, make the relish. Mix together the unsweetened yogurt, mint jelly, cucumber, and freshly chopped mint in a bowl. Cover and chill in the refrigerator until it is required.

5 Drain the burgers on absorbent paper towels. Serve the burgers inside the rolls with sliced tomatoes, cucumber, lettuce, and relish.

Tricolor Chicken & Spinach Lasagne

Serves 4 • CALORIES PER SERVING: 424 • FAT CONTENT PER SERVING: 7.2 G

INGREDIENTS

12 ounces frozen chopped
    spinach, thawed and
    drained
$1/2$ tsp ground nutmeg
1 pound lean, cooked chicken,
    skinned and diced
4 sheets precooked lasagne
    verde
$1^1/2$ tbsp cornstarch
$1^3/4$ cups skim milk

4 tbsp Parmesan cheese,
    freshly grated
salt and pepper

TOMATO SAUCE:
14 ounce can chopped
    tomatoes
1 medium onion, finely
    chopped
1 garlic clove, crushed

$2/3$ cup white wine
3 tbsp tomato paste
1 tsp dried oregano

1 Preheat the oven to
400°F. To make the
tomato sauce, place
the tomatoes in a saucepan
and stir in the onion, garlic,
wine, tomato paste, and
oregano. Bring to a boil and
simmer for 20 minutes,
until thick. Season well.

2 Drain the spinach
again and spread it out
on absorbent paper towels
to make sure that as much

water as possible has been
removed. Layer the spinach
in the base of an ovenproof
baking dish. Sprinkle with
nutmeg and season.

3 Arrange the chicken
over the spinach, and
spoon the tomato sauce on
top. Arrange the sheets of
lasagne over the sauce.

4 Blend the cornstarch
with a little of the milk

to make a paste. Pour the
remaining milk into a pan
and stir in the cornstarch
paste. Heat for 2–3
minutes, stirring, until the
sauce thickens. Season.

5 Spoon the sauce over
the lasagne and transfer
the dish to a cookie sheet.
Sprinkle the grated cheese
over the sauce and bake in
the oven for 25 minutes,
until golden-brown.

Chicken Pasta Bake
with Fennel & Raisins

Serves 4 • CALORIES PER SERVING: 521 • FAT CONTENT PER SERVING: 15.5 G

INGREDIENTS

2 bulbs fennel
2 medium red onions, finely
    shredded
1 tbsp lemon juice
4¹/₂ ounces button mushrooms
1 tbsp olive oil
8 ounces penne (pasta quills)

¹/₃ cup raisins
8 ounces lean, boneless
    cooked chicken,
    skinned and shredded
13 ounces low-fat soft cheese
    with garlic and herbs

4¹/₂ ounces low-fat mozzarella
    cheese, thinly sliced
2 tbsp Parmesan cheese, grated
salt and pepper

1 Preheat the oven to 400°F. Trim the fennel and reserve the green fronds for garnishing. Slice the fennel bulbs thinly. Coat the onion in the lemon juice. Quarter the mushrooms.

2 Heat the oil in a large skillet and sauté the fennel, onion, and mushrooms for 4–5 minutes, stirring, until just softened. Season and transfer the vegetable mixture to a large bowl.

3 Bring a pan of lightly salted water to a boil and cook the penne according to the instructions on the packet until "al dente". Drain and mix the pasta with the vegetables.

4 Stir the raisins and chicken into the pasta mixture. Soften the soft cheese by beating it, then mix into the pasta and chicken—the heat from the pasta should make the cheese melt slightly.

5 Put the mixture into an ovenproof dish and transfer to a cookie sheet. Arrange the mozzarella over the top and sprinkle with the grated Parmesan. Bake in the oven for 20–25 minutes, until golden. Garnish with chopped fennel fronds and serve hot.

Baked Southern-style Chicken

Serves 4 • CALORIES PER SERVING: 402 • FAT CONTENT PER SERVING: 7.4 G

INGREDIENTS

4 baking potatoes, 8 ounces each	$^{1}/_{2}$ tsp paprika	6 tbsp dry white bread crumbs
1 tbsp sunflower oil	$^{1}/_{2}$ tsp dried thyme	salt and pepper
2 tsp coarse sea salt	8 chicken drumsticks, skin removed	
2 tbsp all-purpose flour	1 medium egg, beaten	TO SERVE:
pinch of cayenne pepper	2 tbsp cold water	low-fat coleslaw salad
		corn relish

1 Preheat the oven to 400°F. Wash and scrub the potatoes and cut each into 8 equal portions. Place in a clean plastic bag and add the oil. Seal and shake the bag well to coat.

2 Arrange the potato wedges, skin side down, on a nonstick cookie sheet, sprinkle with the sea salt, and bake in the oven for 30–35 minutes, until they are tender and golden.

3 Meanwhile, mix the flour, cayenne pepper,

paprika, thyme, and salt and pepper to taste on a plate. Press the chicken drumsticks into the seasoned flour to coat.

4 On one plate mix together the egg and water. On another plate sprinkle the bread crumbs. Dip the chicken drumsticks first in the egg, and then in the bread crumbs. Place on a nonstick cookie sheet.

5 Bake the chicken drumsticks alongside the potato wedges for

30 minutes, turning after 15 minutes, until they are tender and cooked through.

6 Drain the potato wedges thoroughly on absorbent paper towels to remove any excess fat. Serve with the chicken, accompanied with low-fat coleslaw and corn relish, if desired.

Lime Chicken Kabobs with Mango Salsa

Serves 4 • CALORIES PER SERVING: 200 • FAT CONTENT PER SERVING: 1.5 G

INGREDIENTS

4 boneless, skinless chicken
    breasts, about 4^1/$_2$ ounces
    each
3 tbsp lime marmalade
1 tsp white wine vinegar
^{1}/$_2$ tsp lime rind, finely grated
1 tbsp lime juice

salt and pepper

TO SERVE:
lime wedges
boiled white rice, sprinkled
    with chili powder

SALSA:
1 small mango
1 small red onion
1 tbsp lime juice
1 tbsp chopped fresh cilantro

1 Slice the chicken breasts into thin pieces and thread onto 8 skewers so that the meat forms an S-shape down each skewer.

2 Preheat the broiler. Arrange the chicken kabobs on the broiler rack. Mix together the marmalade, vinegar, lime rind, and juice. Season with salt and pepper to taste. Brush the dressing generously over the chicken and broil for 5 minutes. Turn the chicken over, brush with the dressing again, and broil for a further 4-5 minutes, until the chicken is cooked through.

3 Meanwhile, prepare the salsa. Peel the mango and slice the flesh off the smooth, central pit, using a sharp knife. Dice the flesh into small pieces and place in a small bowl.

4 Peel and finely chop the onion and mix into the mango, together with the lime juice and chopped cilantro. Season with salt and pepper, cover, and chill until it is required.

5 Transfer the chicken kabobs to serving plates and serve with the salsa, accompanied with wedges of lime and boiled rice sprinkled with a little chili powder.

Sage Chicken & Rice

Serves 4 • CALORIES PER SERVING: 391 • FAT CONTENT PER SERVING: 3.9 G

INGREDIENTS

1 large onion, chopped
1 garlic clove, crushed
2 celery stalks, sliced
2 carrots, diced
2 sprigs fresh sage
1 1/4 cups chicken stock
12 ounces boneless, skinless
  chicken breasts

1 1/3 cups mixed brown and
  wild rice
14 ounce can chopped
  tomatoes
dash of Tabasco sauce
2 medium zucchini, trimmed
  and thinly sliced
3 1/2 ounces lean ham, diced
salt and pepper

fresh sage, to garnish

TO SERVE:
salad greens
crusty bread

1 Place the onion, garlic, celery, carrots, and sprigs of fresh sage in a large saucepan and pour in the chicken stock. Bring to a boil, cover the pan, and simmer for 5 minutes.

2 Cut the chicken into 1-inch cubes. Add the chicken to the pan containing the vegetables, cover the pan, and continue to cook for a further 5 minutes.

3 Stir in the rice and chopped tomatoes. Add a dash of Tabasco sauce to taste and season with salt and pepper to taste. Bring to a boil, cover, and simmer for 25 minutes.

4 Stir in the sliced zucchini and diced ham and continue to cook, uncovered, for a further 10 minutes, stirring occasionally, until the rice is just tender.

5 Remove and discard the sprigs of sage. Garnish with a few sage leaves and serve with a salad greens and fresh crusty bread.

COOK'S TIP

If you do not have fresh sage, use 1 tsp of dried sage in step 1.

Chili Chicken & Corn Meatballs

Serves 4 • CALORIES PER SERVING: 223 • FAT CONTENT PER SERVING: 3 G

INGREDIENTS

1 pound lean ground chicken
4 scallions, trimmed and
    finely chopped, plus extra
    to garnish
1 small red chili, seeded and
    finely chopped
1-inch piece fresh ginger root,
    finely chopped
3$\frac{1}{2}$ ounce can corn (no added
    sugar or salt), drained
salt and white pepper
boiled jasmine rice, to serve

SAUCE:
$\frac{2}{3}$ cup fresh chicken stock
3$\frac{1}{2}$ ounces cubed pineapple
    in natural juice, drained,
    with 4 tbsp reserved juice
1 medium carrot, cut into thin
    strips
1 small red bell pepper, seeded
    and diced, plus extra to
    garnish
1 small green bell pepper,
    seeded and diced
1 tbsp light soy sauce

2 tbsp rice vinegar
1 tbsp superfine sugar
1 tbsp tomato paste
2 tsp cornstarch mixed to a
    paste with 4 tsp cold water

1 To make the meatballs, place the chicken in a bowl and add the scallions, chili, ginger, seasoning, and corn. Mix with your hands.

2 Divide the mixture into 16 portions and form each into a ball. Bring a pan of water to a boil. Put the meatballs on a sheet of parchment in a steamer, set over the water, cover, and steam for 10–12 minutes.

3 To make the sauce, pour the stock and pineapple cubes and juice into a pan and bring to a boil. Add the carrot and bell peppers, cover, and simmer for 5 minutes.

4 Stir in the remaining ingredients and heat through, stirring, until thickened. Season and set aside until required.

5 Drain the meatballs and transfer to a serving plate. Garnish and serve with boiled rice and the sauce.

Crispy-Topped Stuffed Chicken

Serves 4 • CALORIES PER SERVING: 211 • FAT CONTENT PER SERVING: 3.8 G

INGREDIENTS

4 boneless, skinless chicken
  breasts, about 5¹/₂ ounces
  each
4 sprigs fresh tarragon
¹/₂ small orange bell pepper,
  seeded and sliced
¹/₂ small green bell pepper,
  seeded and sliced

¹/₂ ounce whole wheat
  bread crumbs
1 tbsp sesame seeds
4 tbsp lemon juice
1 small red bell pepper, halved
  and seeded
7 ounce can chopped
  tomatoes

1 small red chili, seeded and
  chopped
¹/₄ tsp celery salt
salt and pepper
fresh tarragon, to garnish

1 Preheat the oven to
400°F. Slit the chicken
breasts with a small, sharp
knife to create a pocket in
each. Season inside
each pocket with salt and
pepper to taste.

2 Place a sprig of
tarragon and a few
slices of orange and green
bell peppers in each pocket.
Place the chicken breasts
on a nonstick cookie sheet
and sprinkle with the bread
crumbs and sesame seeds.

3 Spoon 1 tablespoon of
lemon juice over each
chicken breast and bake
in the oven for 35–40
minutes, or until the
chicken is tender and
cooked through.

4 Meanwhile, preheat
the broiler. Arrange the
red bell pepper halves, skin
side up, on the rack and
cook for 5–6 minutes, until
the skin blisters. Leave to
cool for 10 minutes, then
peel off the skins.

5 Put the red bell pepper
in a blender, add the
tomatoes, chili, and celery
salt, and process for a few
seconds. Season to taste.
Alternatively, chop the red
bell pepper and press
through a strainer with the
tomatoes and chili.

6 When the chicken is
cooked, heat the sauce,
spoon a little onto a warm
plate, and arrange a chicken
breast in the center.
Garnish and serve.

Chicken with a Curried Yogurt Crust

Serves 4 • CALORIES PER SERVING: 176 • FAT CONTENT PER SERVING: 2 G

INGREDIENTS

1 garlic clove, crushed
1-inch piece fresh ginger root,
    finely chopped
1 fresh green chili, seeded and
    finely chopped
6 tbsp low-fat unsweetened
    yogurt
1 tbsp tomato paste
1 tsp ground turmeric

1 tsp garam masala
1 tbsp lime juice
4 boneless, skinless chicken
    breasts, each 4¹/₂ ounces
salt and pepper
wedges of lime or lemon,
    to serve

RELISH:
4 medium tomatoes
¹/₄ cucumber
1 small red onion
2 tbsp chopped fresh cilantro

1 Preheat the oven to 375°F. In a small bowl mix together the garlic, ginger, chili, yogurt, tomato paste, turmeric, garam masala, lime juice, and seasoning.

2 Wash and pat dry the chicken breasts with paper towels and place them on a cookie sheet. Brush or spread the spicy yogurt mix over the chicken and bake in the oven for 30–35 minutes until the meat is tender and cooked through.

3 To make the relish, finely chop the tomatoes, cucumber, and onion and mix together with the cilantro. Season with salt and pepper, cover, and chill until required.

4 Drain the cooked chicken on absorbent paper towels and serve hot with the relish. Alternatively, allow to cool, chill for at least 1 hour, and serve sliced as part of a salad.

VARIATION

The spicy yogurt coating would work just as well if spread on a chunky white fish, such as cod fillet. The cooking time should be reduced to 15–20 minutes.

Broiled Chicken with Lemon & Honey

Serves 4 • CALORIES PER SERVING: 403 • FAT CONTENT PER SERVING: 4.7 G

INGREDIENTS

4 boneless, skinless chicken
    breasts, about 4¹/₂ ounces
    each
2 tbsp clear honey
1 tbsp dark soy sauce
1 tsp finely grated lemon rind

1 tbsp lemon juice
salt and pepper

TO GARNISH:
1 tbsp fresh chives, chopped
lemon rind, grated

NOODLES:
8 ounces rice noodles
2 tsp sesame oil
1 tbsp sesame seeds
1 tsp finely grated lemon rind

1 Preheat the broiler. Trim the chicken breasts to remove any excess fat, then wash, and pat dry with absorbent paper towels. Using a sharp knife, score the chicken breasts with a criss-cross pattern on both sides (making sure that you do not cut all the way through the meat).

2 Carefully mix together the honey, soy sauce, lemon rind, and juice in a small bowl, and then season well with a little black pepper.

3 Arrange the chicken breasts on the broiler rack and brush with half of the honey mixture. Cook for 10 minutes, turn over, and brush with the remaining mixture. Cook for a further 8–10 minutes, or until cooked through.

4 Meanwhile, prepare the noodles according to the instructions on the packet. Drain well and transfer to a warm serving bowl. Mix the noodles with the sesame oil, sesame seeds, and the lemon rind. Season with salt and pepper to taste and keep warm.

5 Drain the chicken and serve with a small mound of noodles, garnished with freshly chopped chives and grated lemon rind.

Chicken & Plum Casserole

Serves 4 • CALORIES PER SERVING: 285 • FAT CONTENT PER SERVING: 6.4 G

INGREDIENTS

2 slices lean bacon, chopped
1 tbsp sunflower oil
1 pound skinned, boned chicken thighs, cut into 4 equal strips
1 garlic clove, crushed
6 ounces shallots, halved

8 ounces plums, halved or quartered (if large) and pitted
1 tbsp light brown sugar
²/3 cup dry sherry
2 tbsp plum sauce
2 cups fresh chicken stock

2 tsp cornstarch mixed with 4 tsp cold water
2 tbsp chopped flat-leaf parsley, to garnish
crusty bread, to serve

---

1 In a large, nonstick skillet, dry-fry the bacon for 2–3 minutes, until the juices run out. Remove the bacon from the pan with a slotted spoon, set aside, and keep warm.

2 In the same skillet, heat the sunflower oil and fry the strips of chicken with the garlic and shallots for 4–5 minutes, stirring occasionally, until well browned all over.

3 Return the bacon to the skillet and stir in the plums, sugar, sherry, plum sauce, and stock. Bring to a boil and simmer for 20 minutes, or until the plums have softened and the chicken is completely cooked through.

4 Add the cornstarch mixture to the skillet and cook, stirring occasionally, for a further 2–3 minutes, until the mixture has thickened.

5 Spoon the casserole onto warm serving plates and garnish with chopped parsley. Serve with chunks of bread to mop up the fruity gravy.

VARIATION

Chunks of lean turkey or pork would also go well with this combination of flavors. The cooking time will remain the same.

Orange Turkey with Rice & Green Vegetables

Serves 4 • CALORIES PER SERVING: 354 • FAT CONTENT PER SERVING: 5.5 G

INGREDIENTS

1 tbsp olive oil
1 medium onion, chopped
1 pound skinless lean turkey
   (such as fillet), cut into
   thin strips
1¼ cups unsweetened
   orange juice

1 bay leaf
8 ounces small broccoli florets
1 large zucchini, diced
1 large orange
6 cups cooked brown rice
salt and pepper

1 ounce pitted black olives in
   brine, drained and
   quartered, to garnish

1 Heat the oil in a large skillet and fry the onion and turkey, stirring, for 4–5 minutes, until lightly browned.

2 Pour in the orange juice and add the bay leaf and seasoning. Bring to a boil and simmer for 10 minutes.

3 Meanwhile, bring a large pan of water to a boil and cook the broccoli, covered, for 2 minutes. Add the diced zucchini, bring back to a boil, cover, and cook for 3 minutes (do not overcook). Drain and set aside.

4 Using a sharp knife, peel off the skin and white pith from the orange. Slice down the orange to make thin, round slices, then cut each slice in half.

5 Stir the broccoli, zucchini, rice, and orange slices into the turkey mixture. Gently mix together and heat through for a further 3–4 minutes, until piping hot.

6 Transfer the turkey rice to serving plates and garnish with black olives.

Curried Turkey with Apricots & Golden Raisins

Serves 4 • CALORIES PER SERVING: 418 • FAT CONTENT PER SERVING: 7.9 G

INGREDIENTS

1 tbsp vegetable oil
1 large onion, chopped
1 pound skinless turkey breast, cut into 1 inch cubes
3 tbsp mild curry paste
1¼ cups fresh chicken stock
6 ounces frozen peas

14 ounce can apricot halves in natural juice
⅓ cup golden raisins
6 cups Basmati rice, freshly cooked
1 tsp ground coriander
4 tbsp fresh cilantro, chopped

1 green chili, seeded and sliced
salt and pepper

---

1 Heat the oil in a large saucepan and fry the onion and turkey for 4–5 minutes, until the onion has softened and the turkey is a light golden color.

2 Stir in the curry paste. Pour in the stock, stirring, and bring to a boil. Cover and simmer for 15 minutes. Stir in the peas and bring back to a boil. Cover and simmer for 5 minutes.

3 Drain the apricots, reserving the juice, and cut into thick slices. Add the apricots to the curry, stirring in a little of the juice if the mixture is becoming dry. Add the golden raisins and cook for 2 minutes.

4 Mix the rice with the ground coriander and fresh cilantro, stir in the chili, and season with salt and pepper. Transfer the rice to warm plates and top with the curry.

VARIATION

Peaches can be used instead of the apricots if you prefer. Cook in exactly the same way.

Turkey Loaf with Zucchini & Tomato

Serves 6 • Calories per serving: 179 • Fat content per serving: 2.7 g

INGREDIENTS

1 medium onion, finely
    chopped
1 garlic clove, crushed
2 pounds lean ground turkey
1 tbsp chopped fresh parsley
1 tbsp chopped fresh chives

1 tbsp chopped fresh tarragon
1 medium egg white, lightly
    beaten
1 medium and 1 large zucchini
2 medium tomatoes
salt and pepper

tomato and herb sauce, to
    serve

1 Preheat the oven to 375°F and line a nonstick loaf pan with baking parchment. Place the onion, garlic, and turkey in a bowl, add the herbs, and season to taste. Mix together with your hands, then add the egg white to bind.

2 Press half of the turkey mixture into the base of the pan. Thinly slice the medium zucchini and the tomatoes and arrange the slices over the meat. Top with the rest of the turkey and press down firmly.

3 Cover with a layer of foil and place in a roasting pan. Pour in enough boiling water to come halfway up the sides of the pan. Bake in the oven for 1–1¼ hours, removing the foil for the last 20 minutes of cooking. Test the loaf by inserting a skewer into the center—the juices should run clear.

4 Using a vegetable peeler or hand-held metal cheese slicer, cut the large zucchini into thin slices. Bring a saucepan of water to a boil and blanch the zucchini slices for 1–2 minutes, until just tender. Drain, set aside, and keep warm.

5 Transfer the turkey loaf to a warm platter. Drape the zucchini slices over the loaf and serve with a tomato and herb sauce.

Duck with Kiwi Fruit & Raspberries

Serves 4 • CALORIES PER SERVING: 286 • FAT CONTENT PER SERVING: 8.4 G

INGREDIENTS

1 pound boneless, skinless
duck breasts
2 tbsp raspberry vinegar
2 tbsp brandy
1 tbsp clear honey
1 tsp sunflower oil

salt and pepper

SAUCE:
8 ounces raspberries, thawed
if frozen
1¼ cups rosé wine

2 tsp cornstarch blended with
4 tsp cold water

1 Trim the duck breasts to remove any excess fat. Using a sharp knife, score the flesh in diagonal lines and then pound it with a meat mallet or a covered rolling pin until it is about ¾ inch thick.

2 Place the duck breasts in a shallow dish. Mix together the vinegar, brandy, and honey in a small bowl and spoon it over the duck. Cover and chill in the refrigerator for 1 hour. Preheat the broiler.

3 Drain the duck, reserving the marinade, and place on the broiler rack. Season and brush with oil. Cook for 10 minutes, turn over, season, brush with oil again, and cook for 8–10 minutes, until the meat is cooked through.

4 To make the sauce, reserve 2 ounces raspberries and place the rest in a pan. Add the marinade and the wine. Bring to a boil and simmer for 5 minutes, until reduced.

5 Strain the sauce through a strainer, pressing the raspberries with the back of a spoon. Return the liquid to the pan and add the cornstarch paste. Heat through, stirring, until thickened. Add the reserved raspberries and season.

6 Thinly slice the duck breast and arrange fanned out on serving plates, alternating with slices of kiwi fruit. Pour on the sauce and serve.

Roast Duck with Apples & Apricots

Serves 4 • CALORIES PER SERVING: 313 • FAT CONTENT PER SERVING: 6.5 G

INGREDIENTS

4 duckling portions, 12 ounces each	juice of 1 lemon	SAUCE:
4 tbsp dark soy sauce	2 tbsp clear honey	14 ounce can apricots, in natural juice
2 tbsp light brown sugar	few bay leaves	4 tbsp sweet sherry
2 red-skinned apples	salt and pepper	
2 green-skinned apples	assorted fresh vegetables, to serve	

1 Preheat the oven to 375°F. Wash the duck and trim away any excess fat. Place on a wire rack over a roasting pan and prick all over with a fork.

2 Brush the duck with the soy sauce. Sprinkle on the sugar and season with pepper. Cook in the oven, basting occasionally, for 50–60 minutes, until the meat is cooked through—the juices should run clear when a skewer is inserted into the thickest part of the meat.

3 Meanwhile, core the apples and cut each into 6 wedges. Place in a bowl and mix with the lemon juice and honey. Transfer to a small roasting pan, add a few bay leaves, and season. Cook alongside the duck, basting occasionally, for 20–25 minutes, until tender. Discard the bay leaves.

4 To make the sauce, place the apricots in a blender or food processor, together with the juice from the can and the sherry. Process for a few seconds until smooth. Alternatively, mash the apricots with a fork until smooth and mix with the juice and sherry.

5 Just before serving, heat the apricot paste in a pan. Remove the skin from the duck (if wished) and pat the flesh with paper towels to absorb any fat.

6 Serve the duck with the apple wedges and the sauce, and accompanied with vegetables.

Fish
& Shellfish

Naturally low in fat, yet rich in minerals and proteins, white fish and shellfish will be regular and important ingredients in any low-fat diet. There are so many flavors and textures available that the possible combinations are endless.

White fish, such as monkfish, haddock, cod, and turbot, are widely available and easy to cook. Shellfish, too, are low in fat and rich in flavor, and they can be cooked in a variety of ways to produce mouthwatering, low-fat dishes. Some fish—salmon, tuna, trout, and mackerel, for example—are oily and should be eaten in moderation. They are rich in the fat-soluble vitamins A and D, however, and it is also believed that the oil in these fish is beneficial in breaking down cholesterol in the bloodstream.

Use this versatile ingredient in recipes that will soon become standards in your repertoire, from comforting Shrimp and Tuna Pasta Bake and Fish Cakes with Piquant Tomato Sauce, to sophisticated Five-spice Salmon with Ginger Stir-fry and Oriental Shellfish Kabobs.

Shrimp & Tuna Pasta Bake

Serves 4 • CALORIES PER SERVING: 470 • FAT CONTENT PER SERVING: 8.5 G

INGREDIENTS

8 ounces tricolor pasta shapes
1 tbsp vegetable oil
1 bunch scallions, trimmed
    and chopped
6 ounces button mushrooms,
    sliced
14 ounce can tuna in water,
    drained and flaked

6 ounces peeled shrimp,
    thawed if frozen
2 tbsp cornstarch
1³/₄ cups skim milk
4 medium tomatoes, sliced
    thinly
1 ounce fresh bread crumbs

1 ounce reduced-fat cheddar
    cheese, grated
salt and pepper

1 Preheat the oven to 375°F. Bring a large pan of water to a boil and cook the pasta according to the instructions on the packet, until it is tender but still firm to the bite. Drain thoroughly.

2 Meanwhile, heat the oil in a skillet and sauté all but a handful of the scallions and all of the mushrooms, stirring, for 4–5 minutes until softened.

3 Place the cooked pasta in a bowl and mix in the scallions, mushrooms, tuna, and shrimp. Set aside and keep warm until required.

4 Blend the cornstarch with a little milk to make a paste. Pour the remaining milk into a saucepan and stir in the paste. Heat, stirring, until the sauce begins to thicken. Season with salt and pepper.

5 Pour the sauce over the pasta mixture and stir until well combined. Transfer to the base of an ovenproof gratin dish and place on a cookie sheet.

6 Arrange the tomato slices over the pasta and sprinkle with the bread crumbs and cheese. Bake for 25–30 minutes until golden. Serve sprinkled with the reserved chopped scallions.

Fish Cakes with Piquant Tomato Sauce

Serves 4 • CALORIES PER SERVING: 320 • FAT CONTENT PER SERVING: 7.5 G

INGREDIENTS

1 pound potatoes, diced
8 ounces haddock fillet
8 ounces trout fillet
1 bay leaf
1³/4 cups fresh fish stock
2 tbsp low-fat unsweetened
    yogurt
4 tbsp fresh snipped chives

2³/4 ounces dry white
    bread crumbs
1 tbsp sunflower oil
salt and pepper
snipped chives, to garnish

TO SERVE:
lemon wedges
salad greens

PIQUANT TOMATO SAUCE:
³/4 cup sieved tomatoes
4 tbsp dry white wine
4 tbsp low-fat unsweetened
    yogurt
chili powder

1 Place the potatoes in a saucepan and cover with water. Bring to a boil and cook for 10 minutes, or until tender. Drain well and mash.

2 Meanwhile, place the fish in a pan with the bay leaf and stock. Bring to a boil and simmer for 7–8 minutes, or until tender. Remove the fish with a slotted spoon and flake the flesh away from the skin.

3 Gently mix the cooked fish with the potato, yogurt, chives, and seasoning. Cool, then cover, and chill for 1 hour.

4 Sprinkle the bread crumbs on a plate. Divide the fish mixture into 8 and form each portion into a patty, about 3 inches in diameter. Press each fish cake into the bread crumbs, coating it all over.

5 Brush a skillet with oil and fry the fish cakes for 6 minutes on each side, or until golden. Drain on paper towels and keep warm.

6 To make the sauce, heat the sieved tomatoes and wine. Season, remove from the heat, and stir in the yogurt. Return to the heat, sprinkle with chili powder, and serve with the fish cakes.

Provençal-style Mussels

Serves 4 • CALORIES PER SERVING: 185 • FAT CONTENT PER SERVING: 6.5 G

INGREDIENTS

1 tbsp olive oil
1 large onion, finely chopped
1 garlic clove, finely chopped
1 small red bell pepper, seeded and finely chopped
sprig of rosemary
2 bay leaves
14 ounce can chopped tomatoes

²/₃ cup white wine
1 zucchini, diced finely
2 tbsp tomato paste
1 tsp superfine sugar
1³/₄ ounces pitted black olives in brine, drained, and chopped
1¹/₂ pounds cooked New Zealand mussels in their shells

1 tsp orange rind
salt and pepper
crusty bread, to serve
2 tbsp chopped, fresh parsley, to garnish

1 Heat the oil in a large saucepan and gently sauté the onion, garlic, and bell pepper for 3–4 minutes, until just softened.

2 Add the sprig of rosemary and the bay leaves to the saucepan with the tomatoes and ⅓ cup of wine. Season with salt and pepper to taste, then bring to a boil, and simmer for about 15 minutes.

3 Stir in the zucchini, tomato paste, sugar, and olives. Simmer for 10 minutes.

4 Meanwhile, bring a pan of water to a boil. Arrange the mussels in a steamer or a large strainer and place over the water. Sprinkle with the remaining wine and the orange rind. Cover and steam until the mussels open (discard any that remain closed).

5 Remove the mussels with a slotted spoon and arrange on a warm serving plate. Discard the herbs and spoon the sauce over the mussels. Garnish with chopped parsley and serve with crusty bread.

Fish & Rice with Dark Rum

Serves 4 • CALORIES PER SERVING: 575 • FAT CONTENT PER SERVING: 4.5 G

INGREDIENTS

1 pound firm white fish fillets
(such as cod or monkfish),
skinned and cut into
1-inch cubes
2 tsp ground cumin
2 tsp dried oregano
2 tbsp lime juice
2/3 cup dark rum
1 tbsp dark brown sugar
3 garlic cloves, finely chopped
1 large onion, chopped

1 medium red bell pepper,
seeded and sliced into
rings
1 medium green bell pepper,
seeded and sliced into
rings
1 medium yellow bell pepper,
seeded and sliced into
rings
5 cups fish stock
2 cups long-grain rice

salt and pepper
crusty bread, to serve

TO GARNISH:
fresh oregano leaves
lime wedges

1 Place the cubes of fish in a bowl and add the cumin, oregano, salt, pepper, lime juice, rum, and sugar. Mix well, cover the bowl, and chill for about 2 hours.

2 Meanwhile, place the garlic, onion, and bell peppers in a large saucepan. Pour in the stock and stir in the rice. Bring to a boil, cover, and cook for 15 minutes.

3 Gently add the fish and the marinade juices to the pan. Bring back to a boil and simmer, uncovered, stirring occasionally but taking care not to break up the fish, for 10 minutes, or until the fish is cooked and the rice is tender.

4 Season and transfer to a serving plate. Garnish with oregano and lime wedges and serve.

VARIATION

If you prefer, use unsweetened orange juice in the marinade instead of the rum.

Seafood Stir-fry

Serves 4 • CALORIES PER SERVING: 205 • FAT CONTENT PER SERVING: 6.5 G

INGREDIENTS

3¹/₂ ounces small, thin
    asparagus spears, trimmed
1 tbsp sunflower oil
1-inch piece fresh ginger root,
    cut into thin strips
1 medium leek, shredded
2 medium carrots, julienned

3¹/₂ ounces baby corn cobs,
    quartered lengthwise
2 tbsp light soy sauce
1 tbsp oyster sauce
1 tsp clear honey
1 pound cooked, assorted
    shellfish, thawed if frozen

freshly cooked egg noodles,
    to serve

TO GARNISH:
4 large cooked shrimp
small bunch fresh chives,
    freshly snipped

1 Bring a small pan of water to a boil and blanch the asparagus for 1–2 minutes. Drain, set aside, and keep warm.

2 Heat the oil in a wok or large skillet and stir-fry the ginger, leek, carrot, and corn for 3 minutes.

3 Add the soy sauce, oyster sauce, and honey to the wok or skillet. Stir in the shellfish and continue to stir-fry for

2–3 minutes until the vegetables are just tender and the shellfish is thoroughly heated through. Add the blanched asparagus to the wok or skillet and stir-fry for about 2 minutes.

4 To serve, pile the cooked noodles onto 4 warm serving plates and spoon the seafood and vegetable stir-fry on top. Serve garnished with a large shrimp and freshly snipped chives.

COOK'S TIP

When you are preparing dense vegetables, such as carrots and other root vegetables, for stir-frying, slice them into thin, evenly sized pieces so that they cook quickly and at the same rate. Delicate vegetables, such as bell peppers, leeks, and scallions, do not need to be cut as thinly.

Smoky Fish Pie

Serves 4 • CALORIES PER SERVING: 510 • FAT CONTENT PER SERVING: 6 G

INGREDIENTS

2 pounds smoked haddock or
   cod fillets
2¹/₂ cups skim milk
2 bay leaves
4 ounces button mushrooms,
   quartered
4 ounces frozen peas

4 ounces frozen corn kernels
1¹/₂ pounds potatoes, diced
5 tbsp low-fat unsweetened
   yogurt
4 tbsp chopped fresh parsley
2 ounces smoked salmon,
   sliced into thin strips

3 tbsp cornstarch
1 ounce smoked cheese,
   grated
salt and pepper

1 Preheat the oven to 400°F. Place the fish in a pan and add the milk and bay leaves. Bring to a boil, cover, and then simmer for 5 minutes.

2 Add the mushrooms, peas, and corn to the pan, bring back to a simmer, cover, and cook for 5–7 minutes. Let cool.

3 Place the potatoes in a pan, cover with water, boil, and cook for 8 minutes. Drain and mash with a fork or a masher. Stir in the yogurt, parsley, and seasoning. Set aside.

4 Using a slotted spoon, remove the fish from the pan. Flake the cooked fish away from the skin and place in an ovenproof gratin dish. Reserve the cooking liquid.

5 Drain the vegetables, reserving the cooking liquid, and gently stir into the fish, together with the salmon strips.

6 Blend a little cooking liquid into the cornstarch to make a paste. Transfer the rest of the liquid to a saucepan and add the paste. Heat through, stirring, until thickened. Discard the bay leaves and season to taste.

7 Pour the sauce over the fish and vegetables. Spoon the mashed potato on top, covering the fish, sprinkle with cheese, and bake for 25–30 minutes. Serve.

Seafood Spaghetti

Serves 4 • CALORIES PER SERVING: 400 • FAT CONTENT PER SERVING: 7 G

INGREDIENTS

2 tsp olive oil
1 small red onion, finely
    chopped
1 tbsp lemon juice
1 garlic clove, crushed
2 celery stalks, finely chopped
²/₃ cup fresh fish stock
²/₃ cup dry white wine
small bunch fresh tarragon

1 pound fresh mussels,
    prepared
8 ounces fresh shrimp, peeled
    and deveined
8 ounces baby squid, cleaned,
    trimmed, and sliced into
    rings
8 small cooked crab claws,
    cracked and peeled

8 ounces spaghetti
salt and pepper
2 tbsp chopped fresh tarragon,
    to garnish

1 Heat the oil in a pan and sauté the onion with the lemon juice, garlic, and celery for 3–4 minutes, until softened.

2 Pour in the stock and wine. Bring to a boil and add the tarragon and mussels. Cover and simmer for 5 minutes. Add the shrimp, squid, and crab claws to the pan, mix together, and cook for 3–4 minutes, until the mussels have opened, the shrimp are pink, and the squid is opaque. Discard any mussels that have not opened, and the tarragon.

3 Meanwhile, cook the spaghetti in a saucepan of boiling water according to the instructions on the packet. Drain well.

4 Add the spaghetti to the shellfish mixture and toss together. Season.

5 Transfer to warm serving plates and spoon the cooking juices on top. Serve garnished with freshly chopped tarragon.

COOK'S TIP

Crab claws contain lean crabmeat. Ask your fish store to crack the claws for you, leaving the pincers intact, because the shell is very tough.

Chili- & Crab-stuffed Red Snapper

Serves 4 • CALORIES PER SERVING: 120 • FAT CONTENT PER SERVING: 1 G

INGREDIENTS

4 red snappers, cleaned and
    scaled, 6 ounces each
2 tbsp dry sherry
salt and pepper
stir-fried shredded vegetables,
    to serve

STUFFING:
1 small red chili
1 garlic clove
1 scallion
1/2 tsp finely grated lime rind
1 tbsp lime juice

3 1/2 ounces white crabmeat,
    flaked

TO GARNISH:
wedges of lime
red chilli strips

1 Rinse the fish and pat
dry on absorbent paper
towels. Season inside and
out and place in a shallow
dish. Spoon the sherry over
the fish and set aside.

2 Meanwhile, make the
stuffing. Carefully
halve, seed, and finely chop
the chili. Place the chili in a
small bowl.

3 Peel and finely chop
the garlic. Trim and
finely chop the scallion.
Add to the chili together
with the grated lime rind,

lime juice, and the flaked
crabmeat. Season with salt
and pepper to taste and
combine. Spoon some of
the stuffing into the cavity
of each fish.

4 Bring a large saucepan
of water to a boil.
Arrange the fish in a
steamer lined with baking
parchment or in a large
strainer and place over a
boiling water. Cover and
steam for 10 minutes. Turn
the fish over and steam for
a further 10 minutes, or
until the fish is cooked.

5 Drain the fish and
transfer to serving
plates. Garnish with
wedges of lime and serve
with stir-fried vegetables.

COOK'S TIP

*Always wash your hands
thoroughly after handling
chilies, as they can irritate
your skin and eyes.*

Citrus Fish Kabobs

Serves 4 • CALORIES PER SERVING: 335 • FAT CONTENT PER SERVING: 14.5 G

INGREDIENTS

1 pound firm white fish fillets (such as cod or monkfish)	1 bunch fresh bay leaves	TO SERVE:
1 pound thick salmon fillet	1 tsp finely grated lemon rind	crusty bread
2 large oranges	3 tbsp lemon juice	mixed salad
1 pink grapefruit	2 tsp clear honey	
	2 garlic cloves, crushed	
	salt and pepper	

1 Skin the white fish and the salmon, rinse, and pat dry on absorbent paper towels. Cut each fillet into 16 pieces.

2 Using a sharp knife, remove the skin and pith from the oranges and grapefruit. Cut out the segments of flesh, removing all remaining traces of the pith and dividing membrane.

3 Thread the pieces of fish alternately with the orange and grapefruit segments and the bay leaves onto 8 skewers. Place the kabobs in a shallow dish.

4 Mix together the lemon rind and juice, the honey, and garlic. Pour over the kabobs and season. Cover and chill for 2 hours, turning occasionally.

5 Preheat the broiler. Remove the kabobs from the marinade and place on the rack. Cook for 7–8 minutes, turning once, until completely cooked through.

6 Drain the kabobs thoroughly, transfer to serving plates, and serve with crusty bread and a fresh salad.

VARIATION

This dish makes an unusual starter. Try it with any firm fish—shark or swordfish, for example—or with tuna for a meatier texture.

Seafood Pizza

Serves 4 • Calories per serving: 315 • Fat content per serving: 7 g

INGREDIENTS

5 ounces standard
    pizza base mix
4 tbsp chopped fresh dill
    or 2 tbsp dried dill
fresh dill, to garnish

SAUCE:
1 large red bell pepper

14 ounce can chopped
    tomatoes with onion and
    herbs
3 tbsp tomato paste
salt and pepper

TOPPING:
12 ounces assorted cooked
    seafood, thawed if frozen

1 tbsp capers in brine, drained
1 ounce pitted black olives in
    brine, drained
1 ounce low-fat mozzarella
    cheese, grated
1 tbsp grated, fresh Parmesan
    cheese

1 Preheat the oven to 400°F. Place the pizza base mix in a bowl and stir in the dill. Make the dough according to the instructions on the packet.

2 Press the dough into a round measuring 10 inches across on a cookie sheet lined with parchment. Set aside to rise.

3 Preheat the broiler. To make the sauce, halve and seed the bell pepper and arrange on a broiler rack. Cook for 8–10 minutes, until softened and charred. Leave to cool slightly, peel off the skin, and chop the flesh.

4 Place the tomatoes and bell pepper in a saucepan. Bring to a boil and simmer for 10 minutes. Gradually stir in the tomato paste and season with salt and pepper to taste.

5 Spread the sauce over the pizza base and top with the seafood. Sprinkle with the capers and olives, top with the grated cheeses, and bake for 25–30 minutes. Garnish with sprigs of dill and serve hot.

Pan-seared Halibut with Red Onion Relish

Serves 4 • CALORIES PER SERVING: 250 • FAT CONTENT PER SERVING: 8 G

INGREDIENTS

1 tsp olive oil
4 halibut steaks, skinned,
  6 ounces each
1/2 tsp cornstarch mixed with
  2 tsp cold water
salt and pepper

2 tbsp fresh chives, snipped,
  to garnish

RED ONION RELISH:
2 medium red onions
6 shallots
1 tbsp lemon juice

2 tsp olive oil
2 tbsp red wine vinegar
2 tsp superfine sugar
2/3 cup fresh fish stock

1 To make the relish, peel and thinly shred the onions and shallots. Place in a small bowl and toss in the lemon juice.

2 Heat the oil in a pan and sauté the onions and shallots for 3–4 minutes, or until just softened.

3 Add the vinegar and sugar and continue to cook for 2 minutes over a high heat. Pour in the stock and season with salt and pepper to taste. Bring to a boil and simmer gently for a further 8–9 minutes, until the sauce has thickened and is slightly reduced.

4 Brush a nonstick, ridged skillet with oil and heat until hot. Press the fish steaks into the pan to seal, lower the heat, and cook for 4 minutes. Turn the fish over and cook for 4–5 minutes, until cooked through. Drain on paper towels and keep warm.

5 Stir the cornstarch paste into the onion sauce and heat through, stirring, until thickened. Season to taste.

6 Pile the relish onto 4 warm serving plates and place a halibut steak on top of each. Garnish with chives and pepper.

Five-spice Salmon with Ginger Stir-fry

Serves 4 • CALORIES PER SERVING: 295 • FAT CONTENT PER SERVING: 18 G

INGREDIENTS

4 salmon fillets, skinned,
    4 ounces each
2 tsp five-spice powder
1 large leek
1 large carrot
4 ounces snow peas

1-inch piece fresh ginger root
2 tbsp ginger wine
2 tbsp light soy sauce
1 tbsp vegetable oil
salt and pepper

TO GARNISH:
leek, shredded
fresh ginger root, shredded
carrot, shredded

1 Wash the salmon and pat dry on absorbent paper towels. Rub the five-spice powder into both sides of the fish and season with salt and pepper to taste. Set aside until required.

2 Using a sharp knife, trim the leek, slice it down the center, and rinse under cold water to remove any dirt. Finely shred the leek. Peel the carrot and cut it into very thin strips. Top and tail the snow peas and cut them into shreds. Peel the ginger and slice it thinly into strips.

3 Place all of the vegetables into a large bowl and toss in the ginger wine and 1 tablespoon of soy sauce. Set aside.

4 Preheat the broiler. Place the salmon fillets on the rack and brush with the remaining soy sauce. Cook for 2–3 minutes on each side, until completely cooked through.

5 While the salmon is cooking, heat the oil in a nonstick wok or large skillet and stir-fry the vegetables for 5 minutes, until just tender. Ensure that you do not overcook the vegetables—they should still have bite. Transfer to serving plates.

6 Drain the salmon on paper towels and serve on a bed of stir-fried vegetables. Garnish with shredded leek, ginger, and carrot and serve.

Oriental Shellfish Kabobs

Makes 12 • CALORIES PER SERVING: 100 • FAT CONTENT PER SERVING: 2.5 G

INGREDIENTS

12 ounces raw tiger shrimp, peeled leaving tails intact
12 ounces scallops, cleaned, trimmed, and halved (quartered if large)
1 bunch scallions, sliced into 1-inch pieces
1 medium red bell pepper, seeded and cubed

3$^{1}/_{2}$ ounces baby corn cobs, trimmed and sliced into $^{1}/_{2}$-inch pieces
3 tbsp dark soy sauce
$^{1}/_{2}$ tsp hot chili powder
$^{1}/_{2}$ tsp ground ginger
1 tbsp sunflower oil
1 red chili, seeded and sliced

DIP:
4 tbsp dark soy sauce
4 tbsp dry sherry
2 tsp clear honey
1-inch piece fresh ginger root, peeled and grated
1 scallion, trimmed and sliced very finely

1 Soak 12 wooden skewers in cold water for 10 minutes to prevent them from burning.

2 Divide the shrimp, scallops, scallions, bell pepper, and baby corn cobs into 12 portions and thread onto the cooled wooden skewers. Cover the ends with foil so that they do not burn, and place in a shallow dish.

3 Mix the soy sauce, chili powder, and ground ginger and coat the shellfish and vegetable kabobs. Cover and chill for about 2 hours.

4 Preheat the broiler. Arrange the kabobs on the rack, brush the shellfish and vegetables with oil, and cook for 2–3 minutes on each side, until the shrimp turn pink, the scallops

become opaque, and the vegetables are soft.

5 Mix together the dip ingredients and set aside.

6 Remove the foil and transfer the kabobs to a warm serving platter. Garnish with sliced chili and serve with the dip.

Tuna Steaks with Fragrant Spices & Lime

Serves 4 • CALORIES PER SERVING: 200 • FAT CONTENT PER SERVING: 3.5 G

INGREDIENTS

4 tuna steaks, 6 ounces each	1 tsp ground cumin	TO SERVE:
1/2 tsp finely grated lime rind	1 tsp ground coriander	avocado relish (see Cook's Tip)
1 garlic clove, crushed	pepper	lime wedges
2 tsp olive oil	1 tbsp lime juice	tomato wedges
	fresh cilantro, to garnish	

1 Trim the skin from the tuna steaks, rinse, and pat dry on absorbent paper towels.

2 In a small bowl, mix together the lime rind, garlic, olive oil, cumin, ground coriander, and pepper to make a paste.

3 Spread the paste thinly on both sides of the tuna. Heat a nonstick, ridged skillet until hot and press the tuna steaks into the pan to seal them.

Lower the heat and cook for 5 minutes. Turn the fish over and cook for a further 4–5 minutes, until the fish is cooked through. Drain on absorbent paper towels and transfer to a warm serving plate.

4 Sprinkle the lime juice and chopped cilantro over the fish.

5 Serve with freshly made avocado relish (see Cook's Tip), lime wedges and tomato wedges.

COOK'S TIP

For low-fat avocado relish to serve with tuna, peel and remove the pit from one small ripe avocado. Toss in 1 tbsp lime juice. Mix in 1 tbsp freshly chopped cilantro and 1 small finely chopped red onion. Stir in some chopped fresh mango or a chopped medium tomato and season with salt and pepper to taste.

Baked Trout Mexican-style

Serves 4 • CALORIES PER SERVING: 235 • FAT CONTENT PER RECIPE: 5.5 G

INGREDIENTS

4 trout, 8 ounces each
1 small bunch fresh cilantro
4 shallots, finely shredded
1 small yellow bell pepper, seeded and very finely chopped

1 small red bell pepper, seeded and very finely chopped
2 green chilies, seeded and finely chopped
1–2 red chilies, seeded and finely chopped
1 tbsp lemon juice

1 tbsp white wine vinegar
2 tsp superfine sugar
salt and pepper
fresh cilantro, to garnish
salad leaves, to serve

1 Preheat the oven to 350°F. Wash the trout and pat dry with absorbent paper towels. Season the cavities and fill them with a few cilantro leaves.

2 Place the fish side by side in a shallow ovenproof dish. Sprinkle on the shallots, bell peppers, and chilies.

3 Mix together the lemon juice, vinegar, and sugar in a bowl. Spoon over the trout and season with salt and pepper to taste. Cover the dish and bake for 30 minutes, or until the fish is tender and the flesh is opaque.

4 Remove the fish with a fish slice and drain thoroughly. Transfer the fish to warm serving plates and spoon the cooking juices over the fish. Garnish with fresh cilantro and serve immediately with chili bean rice, if you wish (see Cook's Tip) and salad leaves.

COOK'S TIP

To make chili bean rice to serve with this recipe, cook 1¼ cups long-grain white rice in boiling water. Drain and return to the pan. Drain and rinse a 14 ounce can kidney beans and stir into the rice along with 1 tsp each of ground cumin and ground coriander. Stir in 4 tbsp freshly chopped cilantro and season to taste.

Vegetables & Salads

All too frequently, leaf vegetables are overcooked and limp, with all the goodness and flavor boiled out, while salads are often nothing more than a dismal leaf or two of pale green lettuce with a slice of tomato and a dry ring of onion. Make the most of the wonderful range of fresh produce that is available in our shops and markets.

Steam broccoli and cabbage so that they are colorful and crunchy. Enjoy the wonderfully appetizing shades of orange and yellow bell peppers and the almost unbelievable purple-brown of eggplant. Try grating root vegetables—carrots and daikon or mooli—to add flavor and texture to garnishes and casseroles. Look for red and curly lettuces to bring excitement to an enticing summer salad. Use sweet baby tomatoes in salads and on skewers, and raid your garden and windowsill for sprigs of fresh mint and basil leaves.

Nuts and seeds are high in fat, so both should be used in moderation. However, they are a valuable source of protein and minerals, and vegetarians and vegans in particular need to ensure that their diets contain these valuable ingredients.

Vegetable Spaghetti with Lemon Dressing

Serves 4 • CALORIES PER SERVING: 330 • FAT CONTENT PER SERVING: 2.5 G

INGREDIENTS

8 ounces celery root
2 medium carrots
2 medium leeks
1 small red bell pepper
1 small yellow bell pepper
2 garlic cloves
1 tsp celery seeds

1 tbsp lemon juice
10$\frac{1}{2}$ ounces spaghetti
celery leaves, chopped, to
    garnish

LEMON DRESSING:
1 tsp finely grated lemon rind

1 tbsp lemon juice
4 tbsp low-fat unsweetened
    yogurt
2 tbsp snipped fresh chives
salt and pepper

1 Peel the celery root and carrots and cut them into thin matchsticks, using a sharp knife. Place the celery root and carrots in a bowl. Trim and slice the leeks, rinse to flush out any trapped dirt, then shred finely. Halve, seed, and slice the bell peppers. Peel and thinly slice the garlic. Add all of the vegetables to the bowl containing the celery root and the carrots.

2 Toss the vegetables with the celery seeds and lemon juice.

3 Bring a large saucepan of water to a boil and cook the spaghetti according to the instructions on the packet. Drain and keep warm.

4 Meanwhile, bring another large saucepan of water to a boil, put the vegetables in a steamer or strainer and place over the boiling water. Cover and steam for 6–7 minutes or until tender.

5 When the spaghetti and vegetables are cooked, mix the ingredients for the lemon dressing together.

6 Transfer the spaghetti and vegetables to a warm serving bowl and mix with the dressing. Garnish with celery leaves and serve.

Pesto Pasta

Serves 4 • CALORIES PER SERVING: 350 • FAT CONTENT PER SERVING: 4.5 G

INGREDIENTS

8 ounces crimini mushrooms, sliced
3/4 cup fresh vegetable stock
6 ounces asparagus, trimmed and cut into 2-inch lengths
10 1/2 ounces green and white tagliatelle
14 ounces canned artichoke hearts, drained and halved

bread sticks, to serve

TO GARNISH:
basil leaves, shredded
Parmesan shavings

PESTO:
2 large garlic cloves, crushed
1/2 ounce fresh basil leaves, washed
6 tbsp low-fat unsweetened yogurt
2 tbsp freshly grated Parmesan cheese
salt and pepper

1 Place the sliced mushrooms in a saucepan along with the stock. Bring to a boil, cover, and simmer for 3–4 minutes, until just tender. Drain and set aside.

2 Bring a small saucepan of water to a boil and cook the asparagus for 3–4 minutes, until just tender. Drain and set aside until required.

3 Bring a large pan of lightly salted water to a boil and cook the tagliatelle according to the instructions on the packet. Drain, return to the pan, and keep warm.

4 Meanwhile, make the pesto. Place all of the ingredients in a blender or food processor and process for a few seconds until smooth. Alternatively, finely chop the basil and mix all the ingredients together.

5 Add the mushrooms, asparagus, and artichoke hearts to the pasta and cook, stirring, over a low heat for 2–3 minutes. Remove from the heat, mix with the pesto, and transfer to a warm bowl. Garnish with shredded basil leaves and Parmesan shavings and serve with bread sticks.

Rice-stuffed Mushrooms

Serves 4 • Calories per serving: 315 • Fat content per serving: 6 g

INGREDIENTS

4 large flat mushrooms
3 1/2 ounces assorted exotic
   mushrooms, sliced
4 dry-pack, sun-dried
   tomatoes, shredded
2/3 cup dry red wine

4 scallions, trimmed and
   finely chopped
1 1/2 cups cooked red rice
2 tbsp freshly grated
   Parmesan cheese

4 thick slices whole grain or
   whole wheat bread
salt and pepper
scallion, shredded,
   to garnish

1 Preheat the oven to 375°F. Peel the flat mushrooms, pull out the stalks, and set aside. Finely chop the stalks and place in a saucepan.

2 Add the exotic mushrooms to the saucepan, along with the tomatoes and red wine. Bring to a boil, cover, and simmer gently for 2–3 minutes, until just tender. Drain, reserving the cooking liquid, and place in a small bowl.

3 Gently stir in the chopped scallions and cooked rice. Season well and spoon into the flat mushrooms, pressing the mixture down gently. Sprinkle with the grated Parmesan cheese.

4 Arrange the mushrooms in an ovenproof baking dish and pour the reserved cooking juices around them. Bake in the oven for 20–25 minutes, until they are just cooked.

5 Meanwhile, preheat the broiler. Trim the crusts from the bread and toast on each side until lightly browned.

6 Drain the mushrooms and place each one on a piece of toasted bread. Garnish with scallions and serve at once.

Biryani with Caramelized Onions

Serves 4 • CALORIES PER SERVING: 365 • FAT CONTENT PER SERVING: 4.5 G

INGREDIENTS

1 cup Basmati rice, rinsed	8 ounces cauliflower, broken	CARAMELIZED ONIONS:
1/3 cup red lentils, rinsed	into small florets	2 tsp vegetable oil
1 bay leaf	1 large carrot, diced	1 medium red onion, shredded
6 cardamom pods, split	3 1/2 ounces frozen peas	1 medium onion, shredded
1 tsp ground turmeric	2 ounces golden raisins	2 tsp superfine sugar
6 cloves	2 1/2 cups fresh vegetable	
1 tsp cumin seeds	stock	
1 cinnamon stick, broken	salt and pepper	
1 onion, chopped	nan bread, to serve	

1 Place the rice, lentils, bay leaf, spices, onion, cauliflower, carrot, peas, and golden raisins in a large saucepan. Season with salt and pepper and mix well.

2 Pour in the stock, bring to a boil, cover, and simmer for 15 minutes, stirring occasionally, until the rice is tender. Remove from the heat and let stand, covered, for 10 minutes to allow the stock to be absorbed. Discard the bay leaf, cardamom pods, cloves, and cinnamon stick.

3 Meanwhile, make the caramelized onions. Heat the oil in a skillet and sauté the onions over a medium heat for 3–4 minutes until just softened. Add the superfine sugar, raise the heat, and cook, stirring occasionally, for a further 2–3 minutes, until the onions are just golden.

4 Gently mix the rice and vegetables and transfer to warm serving plates. Spoon the caramelized onion on top, and serve with warmed nan bread.

Soft Pancakes with Stir-fried Vegetables & Bean Curd

Serves 4 • CALORIES PER SERVING: 215 • FAT CONTENT PER SERVING: 8.5 G

INGREDIENTS

1 tbsp vegetable oil
1 garlic clove, crushed
1-inch piece fresh ginger root, grated
1 bunch scallions, trimmed and shredded lengthwise
3$^1/_2$ ounces snow peas, topped, tailed, and shredded
8 ounces bean curd, drained and cut into $^1/_2$-inch pieces
2 tbsp dark soy sauce, plus extra to serve

2 tbsp hoisin sauce, plus extra to serve
2 ounces canned bamboo shoots, drained
2 ounces canned water chestnuts, drained and sliced
3$^1/_2$ ounces bean sprouts
1 small red chili, seeded and thinly sliced
1 small bunch fresh chives
12 soft Chinese pancakes

TO SERVE:
shredded Chinese cabbage leaves
1 cucumber, sliced
strips of red chili

1 Heat the oil in a nonstick wok or a large skillet and stir-fry the garlic and ginger for 1 minute. Add the scallions, snow peas, bean curd, soy sauce, and hoisin sauce to the wok or skillet. Stir-fry the vegetables for about 2 minutes.

2 Add the bamboo shoots, water chestnuts, bean sprouts, and red chili to the wok or skillet. Stir-fry for 2 minutes, until the vegetables are just tender, but still have bite. Snip the chives into 1-inch lengths and stir them into the mixture in the wok or skillet.

3 Meanwhile, heat the pancakes according to the instructions on the packet and keep warm.

4 Divide the vegetables and bean curd among the pancakes and roll up. Serve with the Chinese cabbage and extra sauce.

Char-grilled Mediterranean Vegetable Kabobs

Makes 8 • Calories per serving: 65 • Fat content per serving: 2.5 g

INGREDIENTS

1 large red bell pepper
1 large green bell pepper
1 large orange bell pepper
1 large zucchini
4 baby eggplants
2 medium red onions

2 tbsp lemon juice
1 tbsp olive oil
1 garlic clove, crushed
1 tbsp chopped, fresh
    rosemary or 1 tsp dried
salt and pepper

TO SERVE:
cracked wheat, cooked
tomato and olive relish

1 Halve and seed the bell peppers and cut into even sized pieces, about 1 inch wide. Trim the zucchini, cut in half lengthwise, and slice into 1-inch pieces. Place the bell peppers and zucchini into a large bowl and set aside.

2 Using a sharp knife, trim the eggplants and quarter them lengthwise. Peel the onions, then cut each one into 8 even-sized wedges. Add the eggplant and onion pieces to the bowl containing the bell peppers and zucchini.

3 In a small bowl, mix together the lemon juice, olive oil, garlic, rosemary, and salt and pepper to taste. Pour the mixture over the vegetables and stir well to coat.

4 Preheat the broiler. Thread the vegetables onto 8 skewers. Arrange the kabobs on the rack and cook for 10–12 minutes, turning frequently, until the vegetables are lightly charred and just softened.

5 Drain the vegetable kabobs and serve on a bed of cracked wheat accompanied with a tomato and olive relish, if desired.

Stuffed Vegetables Middle Eastern-style

Serves 4 • CALORIES PER SERVING: 330 • FAT CONTENT PER SERVING: 5.5 G

INGREDIENTS

4 large beefsteak tomatoes
4 medium zucchini
2 orange bell peppers
salt and pepper

FILLING:
1 1/4 cups cracked wheat

1/4 cucumber
1 medium red onion
2 tbsp lemon juice
2 tbsp chopped fresh cilantro
2 tbsp chopped fresh mint
1 tbsp olive oil
2 tsp cumin seeds

TO SERVE:
warm pita bread and low-fat
    hummus

1 Preheat the oven to 400°F. Cut off the tops from the tomatoes and reserve. Using a teaspoon, scoop out the tomato pulp, chop, and place in a bowl. Season the tomato shells, then turn them upside down on absorbent paper towels to drain thoroughly.

2 Trim the zucchini and cut a V-shaped groove lengthwise down each one. Finely chop the cut-out zucchini flesh and add to the tomato pulp. Season the zucchini shells with salt and pepper to taste and set aside.

3 Halve the bell peppers. Leaving the stalks intact, cut out the seeds, and discard. Season the bell pepper shells and set aside.

4 To make the filling, soak the cracked wheat according to the instructions on the packet. Finely chop the cucumber and add to the reserved tomato pulp and zucchini mixture.

5 Finely chop the red onion, and add to the vegetable mixture with the lemon juice, herbs, olive oil, cumin, and seasoning, and mix together well.

6 When the wheat has soaked, mix with the vegetables and stuff into the tomato, zucchini, and bell pepper shells. Place the tops on the tomatoes, transfer to a roasting pan, and bake for 20–25 minutes, until cooked through. Drain and serve.

Fragrant Asparagus & Orange Risotto

Serves 4-6 • CALORIES PER SERVING: 420–280 • FAT CONTENT PER SERVING: 7.5–5 G

INGREDIENTS

4 ounces fine asparagus
spears, trimmed
5 cups vegetable stock
2 bulbs fennel
1 ounce low-fat spread
1 tsp olive oil

2 celery stalks, trimmed and
chopped
2 medium leeks, trimmed
and shredded
2 cups arborio rice
3 medium oranges

salt and pepper

1 Bring a small saucepan of water to a boil and cook the asparagus for 1 minute. Drain and set aside until required.

2 Pour the stock into a saucepan and bring to a boil. Reduce the heat to maintain a gentle simmer.

3 Meanwhile, trim the fennel, reserving the fronds, and cut into thin slices. Carefully melt the low-fat spread with the oil in a large saucepan, taking care that the water in the low-fat spread does not evaporate, and gently sauté the fennel, celery, and leeks for 3–4 minutes, until just softened. Add the rice and cook, stirring, for a further 2 minutes, until mixed.

4 Add a ladleful of stock to the pan and cook gently, stirring, until absorbed. Continue ladling the stock into the rice until the rice becomes creamy, thick, and tender. This process will take about 25 minutes and should not be hurried.

5 Finely grate the rind and extract the juice from 1 orange and mix into the rice. Carefully remove the peel and pith from the remaining oranges. Holding the fruit over the saucepan, cut out the orange segments and add to the rice, along with any juice that falls.

6 Stir the orange into the rice, along with the asparagus spears. Season with salt and pepper, garnish with the reserved fennel fronds, and serve.

Spicy Black-eyed Peas

Serves 4 • CALORIES PER SERVING: 445 • FAT CONTENT PER SERVING: 6 G

INGREDIENTS

2 cups black-eyed peas,
soaked overnight in cold
water
1 tbsp vegetable oil
2 medium onions, chopped
1 tbsp clear honey
2 tbsp molasses
4 tbsp dark soy sauce

1 tsp dry mustard powder
4 tbsp tomato paste
2 cups fresh vegetable stock
1 bay leaf
1 sprig each of rosemary,
thyme, and sage
1 small orange
1 tbsp cornstarch

2 medium red bell peppers,
seeded and diced
pepper
2 tbsp chopped fresh flat-leaf
parsley, to garnish
crusty bread, to serve

---

1 Preheat the oven to 300°F. Rinse the peas and place in a saucepan. Cover with water, bring to a boil, and boil rapidly for 10 minutes. Drain and place in an ovenproof casserole dish.

2 Meanwhile, heat the oil in a skillet and sauté the onions for 5 minutes. Stir in the honey, molasses, soy sauce, mustard, and tomato paste. Pour in the stock, bring to a boil, and pour the mixture over the peas.

3 Tie the bay leaf, rosemary, thyme, and sage together with a clean piece of string and add to the pan containing the peas. Using a vegetable peeler, pare off 3 pieces of orange rind. Mix the orange rind into the pea mixture, along with plenty of freshly ground black pepper. Cover and bake for about 1 hour.

4 Extract the juice from the orange and blend with the cornstarch to form a paste. Stir into the peas, along with the red bell peppers. Cover and cook for 1 hour, until the sauce is rich and thick and the peas are tender. Discard the herbs and orange rind.

5 Garnish with chopped parsley and serve with lots of fresh crusty bread.

Mexican-style Pizzas

Serves 4 • CALORIES PER SERVING: 585 • FAT CONTENT PER SERVING: 16 G

INGREDIENTS

4 ready-made individual
  pizza bases
1 tbsp olive oil
7 ounce can chopped
  tomatoes with garlic and
  herbs
2 tbsp tomato paste

7 ounce can kidney beans,
  drained and rinsed
4 ounces corn kernels, thawed
  if frozen
1–2 tsp chili sauce
1 large red onion, shredded

$3^1/2$ ounces reduced-fat
  cheddar cheese, grated
1 large green chili, sliced into
  rings
salt and pepper

1 Preheat the oven to 425°F. Arrange the pizza bases on a cookie sheet and brush them lightly with the oil.

2 In a bowl, mix together the chopped tomatoes, tomato paste, kidney beans, and corn, and add chili sauce to taste. Season with salt and pepper to taste.

3 Spread the tomato and kidney bean mixture evenly over each pizza base

to cover. Top each pizza with shredded onion and sprinkle with some grated cheese and a few slices of green chili according to taste. Bake in the oven for about 20 minutes until the vegetables are tender, the cheese has melted, and the base is crisp and golden.

4 Remove the pizzas from the cookie sheet and transfer to serving plates. Serve immediately.

COOK'S TIP

For a low-fat Mexican-style salad to serve with this pizza, arrange sliced tomatoes, fresh cilantro leaves, and a few slices of a small, ripe avocado. Sprinkle with fresh lime juice and coarse sea salt. Avocados have quite a high oil content, so eat in moderation.

Eggplant Pasta Cake

Serves 6-8 • CALORIES PER SERVING: 290–215 • FAT CONTENT PER SERVING: 7–5 G

INGREDIENTS

1 medium eggplant	1⅓ cups sieved tomatoes	salt and pepper
10½ ounces tricolor pasta shapes	4 tbsp grated Parmesan cheese	
4 ounces low-fat soft cheese with garlic and herbs	1½ tsp dried oregano	
	2 tbsp dry white bread crumbs	

1 Preheat the oven to 375°F. Grease and line an 8 inch round spring-form cake pan.

2 Trim the eggplant and slice lengthwise into slices about ¼ inch thick. Place in a bowl, sprinkle with salt, and set aside for 30 minutes to remove any bitter juices. Rinse well under cold running water and drain.

3 Bring a saucepan of water to a boil and blanch the eggplant slices for 1 minute. Drain and pat dry with paper towels. Set aside until required.

4 Cook the pasta shapes according to the instructions on the packet; for best results, the pasta should be slightly undercooked. Drain well and return to the saucepan. Add the soft cheese to the pan and allow it to melt over the pasta.

5 Stir in the sieved tomatoes, Parmesan cheese, oregano, and salt and pepper to taste. Set aside until required.

6 Arrange the eggplant over the base and sides of the prepared cake pan, overlapping the slices, and making sure there are no gaps between them.

7 Pile the pasta mixture into the pan, packing down well, and sprinkle with the bread crumbs. Bake for 20 minutes and let stand for 15 minutes.

8 Loosen the cake around the edge with a spatula and release from the pan. Turn out eggplant-side up and serve hot.

Mushroom Cannelloni

Serves 4 • CALORIES PER SERVING: 315 • FAT CONTENT PER SERVING: 3.5 G

INGREDIENTS

12 ounces crimini mushrooms, finely chopped
1 medium onion, finely chopped
1 garlic clove, crushed
1 tbsp chopped fresh thyme
1/2 tsp ground nutmeg
4 tbsp dry white wine

4 tbsp fresh white bread crumbs
12 dried "quick-cook" cannelloni
salt and pepper
Parmesan cheese shavings, to garnish (optional)

TOMATO SAUCE:
1 large red bell pepper
3/4 cup dry white wine
2 cups sieved tomatoes
2 tbsp tomato paste
2 bay leaves
1 tsp superfine sugar

1 Preheat the oven to 400°F. Place the mushrooms, onion, and garlic in a pan. Stir in the thyme, nutmeg, and 4 tbsp wine. Bring to a boil, cover, and simmer for 10 minutes. Stir in the bread crumbs to bind the mixture and season. Leave to cool for 10 minutes.

2 Preheat the broiler. For the sauce, halve and seed the bell pepper, place on the broiler rack, and cook for 8–10 minutes, until charred. Let cool.

3 Once the bell pepper has cooled, peel off the charred skin. Chop the flesh and place in a food processor with the wine. Blend until smooth and pour into a pan.

4 Mix the remaining sauce ingredients with the bell pepper and wine and season. Bring to a boil and simmer for 10 minutes. Discard the bay leaves.

5 Cover the base of an ovenproof dish with a thin layer of sauce. Fill the cannelloni with the mushroom mixture and place in the dish. Spoon the remaining sauce on top, cover with foil, and bake for 35–40 minutes. Garnish with shavings of Parmesan (if using) and serve.

Bean Curd & Garbanzo Burgers

Serves 4 • CALORIES PER SERVING: 280 • FAT CONTENT PER SERVING: 9 G

INGREDIENTS

1 small red onion, finely
   chopped
1 garlic clove, crushed
1 tsp ground cumin
1 tsp ground coriander
2 tbsp lemon juice
15 ounce can garbanzo beans,
   drained and rinsed
3 ounces soft silken bean
   curd, drained
4 ounces cooked potato, diced

4 tbsp freshly chopped
   cilantro
2 tbsp all-purpose flour
   (optional)
$2^3/4$ ounces dry brown bread
   crumbs
1 tbsp vegetable oil
burger rolls
2 medium tomatoes, sliced
1 large carrot, grated
salt and pepper

RELISH:
1 tsp sesame seed paste
4 tbsp low-fat unsweetened
   yogurt
1-inch piece cucumber,
   finely chopped
1 tbsp chopped, fresh cilantro
garlic salt, to season

1 Place the onion, garlic, spices, and lemon juice in a pan, bring to a boil, cover, and simmer for 5 minutes until softened.

2 Place the garbanzo beans, bean curd, and potato in a bowl and mash well. Stir in the onion mixture, cilantro, and seasoning, and mix together. Divide into 4 equal portions and form into patties 4 inches across, dusting the hands with flour, if necessary.

3 Sprinkle the bread crumbs onto a plate and press the burgers into the bread crumbs to coat both sides.

4 Heat the oil in a large nonstick skillet and fry the burgers for 5 minutes on each side, until heated through and golden. Drain on paper towels.

5 Meanwhile, mix all of the relish ingredients together in a bowl and chill.

6 Line the rolls with tomato and grated carrot and top each with a burger. Serve with the relish.

Sweet Potato & Leek Patties

Serves 4 • Calories per serving: 385 • Fat content per serving: 6.5 g

INGREDIENTS

2 pounds sweet potato
4 tsp sunflower oil
2 medium leeks, trimmed and
    finely chopped
1 garlic clove, crushed
1-inch piece fresh ginger root,
    finely chopped
7 ounce can corn kernels,
    drained
2 tbsp low-fat unsweetened
    yogurt

2 ounces whole wheat flour
salt and pepper

GINGER SAUCE:
2 tbsp white wine vinegar
2 tsp superfine sugar
1 red chili, seeded and chopped
1-inch piece fresh ginger root,
    cut into thin strips
2 tbsp ginger wine
4 tbsp fresh vegetable stock

1 tsp cornstarch

TO SERVE:
lettuce leaves
scallions, shredded

1 Peel the potatoes and cut into ¾-inch thick pieces. Place in a saucepan, cover with water, and boil for 10–15 minutes. Drain well and mash. Let cool.

2 Heat 2 tsp of oil and sauté the leeks, garlic, and ginger for 2–3 minutes. Stir the leek mixture into the potato with the corn, seasoning, and yogurt.

Form into 8 patties and toss in flour to coat. Chill for 30 minutes.

3 Preheat the broiler. Place the patties on a broiler rack and brush with oil. Broil for 5 minutes, then turn over. Brush with oil and broil for a further 5 minutes, until golden. Drain thoroughly on paper towels.

4 To make the sauce, place the vinegar, sugar, chili, and ginger in a pan. Bring to a boil and simmer for 5 minutes. Stir in the ginger wine. Blend the stock and cornstarch to form a paste and stir into the sauce. Heat through, stirring, until thickened. Transfer the patties to serving plates, spoon over the sauce, and serve.

Ratatouille Vegetable Broil

Serves 4 • CALORIES PER SERVING: 330 • FAT CONTENT PER SERVING: 4 G

INGREDIENTS

2 medium onions	2 14-ounce cans chopped	2³/4 ounces reduced-fat
1 garlic clove	tomatoes	cheddar cheese, grated
1 medium red bell pepper	1 bouquet garni	salt and pepper
1 medium green bell pepper	2 tbsp tomato paste	2 tbsp snipped fresh chives,
1 medium eggplant	2 pounds potatoes	to garnish
2 medium zucchini		

1 Peel and finely chop the onions and garlic. Rinse, seed, and slice the bell peppers. Rinse, trim, and cut the eggplant into small dice. Rinse, trim, and thinly slice the zucchini.

2 Place the onion, garlic, and bell peppers into a large pan. Add the tomatoes and stir in the bouquet garni, tomato paste, and salt and pepper to taste. Bring to a boil, cover, and simmer for 10 minutes, stirring halfway through.

3 Stir in the eggplant and zucchini and cook, uncovered, for 10 minutes, stirring occasionally.

4 Meanwhile, peel the potatoes and cut into 1-inch cubes. Place the potatoes into another saucepan and cover with water. Bring to a boil and cook for 10–12 minutes, until tender. Drain thoroughly with a slotted spoon and set aside.

5 Transfer the vegetables to a heatproof gratin dish. Arrange the cooked potato cubes evenly over the vegetables.

6 Preheat the broiler. Sprinkle grated cheese over the potatoes and place under the broiler for 5 minutes until golden, bubbling, and hot. Serve immediately garnished with snipped chives.

Mussel & Red Bell Pepper Salad

Serves 4 • CALORIES PER SERVING: 175 • FAT CONTENT PER SERVING: 6 G

INGREDIENTS

2 large red bell peppers
12 ounces cooked shelled
    mussels, thawed if frozen
1 head of radicchio
1 ounce arugula leaves
8 cooked New Zealand
    mussels in their shells

DRESSING:
1 tbsp olive oil
1 tbsp lemon juice
1 tsp finely grated lemon rind
2 tsp clear honey
1 tsp French mustard
1 tbsp snipped fresh chives
salt and pepper

TO SERVE:
lemon wedges
crusty bread

1 Preheat the broiler. Halve and seed the bell peppers and place them skin side up on the rack. Cook for 8–10 minutes, until the skin is charred and blistered and the flesh is soft. Let cool for 10 minutes, then peel off the skin.

2 Slice the bell pepper flesh into thin strips and place in a bowl. Gently mix in the shelled mussels and set aside.

3 To make the dressing, mix all of the ingredients until well blended. Mix into the bell pepper and mussel mixture until coated.

4 Remove the central core of the radicchio and shred the leaves. Place in a serving bowl with the arugula leaves and toss together.

5 Spoon the mussel mixture into the center of the leaves and arrange the cooked New Zealand mussels around the edge of the dish. Serve with lemon wedges and crusty bread.

VARIATION

Replace the shelled mussels with peeled shrimp and the New Zealand mussels with large crevettes, if you prefer. Lime could be used instead of lemon for a different citrus flavor.

Sweet & Sour Fish Salad

Serves 4 • Calories per serving: 190 • Fat content per serving: 7 g

INGREDIENTS

8 ounces trout fillets
8 ounces white fish fillets
    (such as haddock or cod)
1¼ cups water
1 stalk lemon grass
2 lime leaves
1 large red chili
1 bunch scallions, trimmed
    and shredded

4 ounces fresh pineapple
    flesh, diced
1 small red bell pepper, seeded
    and diced
1 bunch watercress, washed
    and trimmed
fresh snipped chives, to
    garnish

DRESSING:
1 tbsp sunflower oil
1 tbsp rice wine vinegar
pinch of chili powder
1 tsp clear honey
salt and pepper

1 Rinse the fish, place in a skillet, and add the water. Bend the lemon grass in half to bruise it and add to the pan with the lime leaves. Prick the chili with a fork and add to the pan. Bring to a boil and simmer for 7–8 minutes. Let cool.

2 Drain the fish fillet, discarding the lemon grass, lime leaves and chili. Flake the fish flesh away from the skin, and place in a bowl. Gently stir in the scallions, pineapple, and bell pepper.

3 Arrange the washed watercress on 4 serving plates, spoon the cooked fish mixture on top, and set aside until required.

4 To make the dressing, mix all the ingredients together and season with salt and pepper to taste.

Spoon the dressing over the fish and serve garnished with chives.

VARIATION

This recipe also works very well if you replace the fish with 12 ounces white crabmeat. Add a dash of Tabasco sauce if you like it hot!

Beef & Peanut Salad

Serves 4 • CALORIES PER SERVING: 320 • FAT CONTENT PER SERVING: 14 G

INGREDIENTS

1/2 head Chinese cabbage
   leaves
1 large carrot
4 ounces radishes
31/2 ounces baby corn cobs
1 tbsp ground nut oil
1 red chili, seeded and
   finely chopped

1 clove garlic, finely chopped
12 ounces lean beef (such as
   fillet, sirloin, or rump),
   trimmed and finely
   shredded
1 tbsp dark soy sauce
1 ounce fresh peanuts
   (optional)

red chili, sliced, to garnish

DRESSING:
1 tbsp smooth peanut butter
1 tsp superfine sugar
2 tbsp light soy sauce
1 tbsp sherry vinegar
salt and pepper

1 Finely shred the Chinese cabbage leaves and arrange on a platter. Peel the carrot and cut into thin, matchstick-like strips. Wash, trim, and quarter the radishes, and halve the baby corn cobs lengthwise. Arrange these ingredients around the edge of the dish and set aside.

2 Heat the oil in a nonstick wok or large skillet and stir-fry the chili, garlic, and beef for

5 minutes. Add the dark soy sauce and stir-fry for a further 1–2 minutes until tender and cooked through.

3 Meanwhile, make the dressing. Place all of the ingredients in a small bowl and blend them together until smooth.

4 Place the hot cooked beef in the center of the salad ingredients. Spoon over the dressing and sprinkle with a few

peanuts, if using. Garnish with the slices of red chili and serve the salad immediately.

VARIATION

If preferred, use chicken, turkey, lean pork, or even strips of venison instead of beef in this recipe. Cut off all visible fat before you begin.

Chicken & Spinach Salad

Serves 4 • CALORIES PER SERVING: 225 • FAT CONTENT PER SERVING: 6 G

INGREDIENTS

4 boneless, skinless chicken
  breasts, 5^1/2 ounces each
2 cups fresh chicken stock
1 bay leaf
8 ounces fresh young
  spinach leaves
1 small red onion, shredded

4 ounces fresh raspberries
salt and freshly ground
  pink peppercorns
fresh toasted croûtons, to
  garnish

DRESSING:
4 tbsp low-fat unsweetened
  yogurt
1 tbsp raspberry vinegar
2 tsp clear honey

1 Place the chicken breasts in a skillet. Add the chicken stock and the bay leaf. Bring to a boil, cover, and simmer for 15–20 minutes, turning halfway through, until the chicken is completely cooked through. Allow to cool in the liquid.

2 Arrange the spinach leaves on 4 serving plates and top with the shredded red onion. Cover and leave to chill in the refrigerator.

3 Drain the cooked chicken and pat dry on absorbent paper towels. Slice the chicken breasts thinly and arrange, fanned out, over the spinach and onion. Sprinkle with the raspberries.

4 To make the dressing, mix all the ingredients together in a small bowl.

5 Drizzle a spoonful of dressing over each chicken breast and season with salt and ground pink

peppercorns to taste. Serve the salad with freshly toasted croûtons.

VARIATION

This recipe is delicious with smoked chicken, but it will be more expensive and richer, so use slightly less. It would make an impressive starter for a dinner party.

Pasta Provençale

Serves 4 • Calories per serving: 295 • Fat content per serving: 6 g

INGREDIENTS

8 ounces penne (pasta quills)
1 tbsp olive oil
1 ounce pitted black olives, drained and chopped
1 ounce dry-pack sun-dried tomatoes, soaked, drained, and chopped
14 ounce can artichoke hearts, drained and halved

4 ounces baby zucchini, trimmed and sliced
4 ounces baby plum tomatoes, halved
$3^1/_2$ ounces assorted baby salad greens
salt and pepper
shredded basil leaves, to garnish

DRESSING:
4 tbsp sieved tomatoes
2 tbsp low-fat unsweetened yogurt
1 tbsp unsweetened orange juice
1 small bunch fresh basil, shredded

1 Cook the penne (pasta quills) according to the instructions on the packet. Do not overcook the pasta—it should still have bite. Drain well and return to the pan. Stir in the olive oil, salt and pepper, olives, and sun-dried tomatoes. Let cool.

2 Gently mix the artichokes, zucchini, and plum tomatoes into the cooked pasta. Arrange the salad greens in a large serving bowl.

3 To make the dressing, mix all the ingredients together until well combined and toss into the vegetables and pasta.

4 Spoon the mixture on top of the salad greens and garnish with shredded basil leaves.

VARIATION

For a nonvegetarian version, stir 8 ounces canned tuna in brine, drained and flaked, into the pasta together with the vegetables. Other pasta shapes can be included—try farfalle (bows) and rotelle (spoked wheels).

Root Vegetable Salad

Serves 4 • CALORIES PER SERVING: 150 • FAT CONTENT PER SERVING: 9 G

INGREDIENTS

12 ounces carrots	3$^1/_2$ ounces assorted salad	1 tsp wholegrain mustard
8 ounces daikon (white radish)	greens	$^1/_2$ tsp finely grated orange
4 ounces radishes	1 ounce chopped walnuts	rind
12 ounces celery root		1 tsp celery seeds
1 tbsp orange juice	DRESSING:	salt and pepper
2 celery stalks with leaves,	1 tbsp walnut oil	
washed and trimmed	1 tbsp white wine vinegar	

1 Peel and coarsely grate or very finely shred the carrots, daikon (white radish), and radishes. Set these vegetables aside in separate bowls until required.

2 Peel and coarsely grate or finely shred the celery root and mix with the orange juice.

3 Remove the celery leaves and reserve for garnishing. Finely chop the celery stalks.

4 Divide the salad greens among 4 serving plates and arrange the carrots, daikon (white radish), and radishes in small piles on top. Set aside while you make the dressing.

5 Mix all of the dressing ingredients together and season with salt and pepper to taste. Drizzle a little of the dressing over each salad. Shred the reserved celery leaves and sprinkle over the salad with the chopped walnuts.

COOK'S TIP

Also known as Chinese white radish and mooli, daikon resembles a large white parsnip. It has crisp, slightly pungent flesh, which can be eaten raw or cooked. It is a useful ingredient in stir-fries. Fresh daikon tend to have a stronger flavor than store-bought ones.

Beet & Orange Rice Salad

Serves 4 • CALORIES PER SERVING: 335 • FAT CONTENT PER SERVING: 2.5 G

INGREDIENTS

1⅓ cups long-grain and wild
  rices (see Cook's Tip)
4 large oranges
1 pound cooked beet, peeled
2 heads of chicory
salt and pepper

fresh snipped chives, to
  garnish

DRESSING:
4 tbsp low-fat unsweetened
  yogurt
1 garlic clove, crushed

1 tbsp wholegrain mustard
½ tsp finely grated orange
  rind
2 tsp clear honey

1 Cook the rices according to the instructions on the packet. Drain and set aside to cool.

2 Slice the top and bottom off each orange and remove the skin and pith. Holding the orange over a bowl to catch the juice, carefully slice between each segment. Place the segments in a separate bowl. Cover the juice and chill in the refrigerator until required.

3 Drain the beet if necessary and dice into cubes. Mix with the orange segments, cover, and chill.

4 When the rice has cooled, mix in the reserved orange juice and season with salt and pepper to taste.

5 Line 4 serving bowls or plates with the chicory leaves. Spoon the rice over the leaves and top with the beet and oranges.

6 Mix all the dressing ingredients together and spoon over the salad, or serve separately in a bowl, if preferred. Garnish with fresh snipped chives.

COOK'S TIP

Look for boxes of ready-mixed long-grain and wild rices. Alternatively, you can cook 1 cup white rice and ¼ cup wild rice separately.

Red Hot Slaw

Serves 4 • CALORIES PER SERVING: 200 • FAT CONTENT PER SERVING: 8.5 G

INGREDIENTS

$^1/_2$ small red cabbage
1 large carrot
2 red-skinned apples
1 tbsp lemon juice
1 medium red onion
$3^1/_2$ ounces reduced-fat
    Cheddar cheese, grated

TO GARNISH:
red chili strips
carrot strips

DRESSING:
3 tbsp reduced-calorie
    mayonnaise

3 tbsp low-fat unsweetened
    yogurt
1 garlic clove, crushed
1 tsp paprika
1–2 tsp chili powder
pinch cayenne pepper
    (optional)
salt and pepper

1 Cut the red cabbage in half and remove the central core. Finely shred the leaves and place in a large bowl. Peel and coarsely grate or finely shred the carrot and mix into the cabbage.

2 Core the apples and finely dice, leaving on the skins. Place in another bowl and toss in the lemon juice to prevent the apple browning. Mix the apple into the cabbage and carrot.

3 Peel and finely shred or grate the onion. Stir into the other vegetables, along with the cheese, and mix together.

4 To make the dressing, mix together the mayonnaise, yogurt, garlic, and paprika in a small bowl. Add chili powder according to taste, and the cayenne pepper, if using— remember this will add more spice to the dressing. Season well.

5 Toss the dressing into the vegetables and mix well. Cover and chill in the refrigerator for 1 hour to allow the flavors to develop. Serve garnished with strips of red chili and carrot.

Pasta Niçoise Salad

Serves 4 • Calories per serving: 370 • Fat content per serving: 9 g

INGREDIENTS

8 ounces farfalle (pasta bows)
6 ounces green beans, topped
   and tailed
12 ounces fresh tuna steaks
4 ounces baby plum
   tomatoes, halved
8 anchovy fillets, drained on
   absorbent paper towels

2 tbsp capers in water, drained
1 ounce pitted black olives in
   water, drained
fresh basil leaves, to garnish
salt and pepper

DRESSING:
1 tbsp olive oil
1 garlic clove, crushed
1 tbsp lemon juice
$1/2$ tsp finely grated lemon rind
1 tbsp shredded fresh basil
   leaves

1 Cook the pasta in a pan of lightly salted boiling water according to the instructions on the packet until just cooked. Drain well, set aside, and keep warm.

2 Bring a small saucepan of lightly salted water to a boil and cook the green beans for 5–6 minutes, until just tender. Drain well and toss into the pasta. Set aside and keep warm.

3 Preheat the broiler. Rinse and pat the tuna steaks dry on absorbent paper towels. Season on both sides with black pepper. Place the tuna steaks on the broiler rack and cook for 4–5 minutes on each side, until cooked through.

4 Drain the tuna on absorbent paper towels and flake into bite-size pieces. Toss the tuna into the pasta, along with the

tomatoes, anchovies, capers, and olives. Set aside and keep warm.

5 Meanwhile, prepare the dressing. Mix all the ingredients together and season well. Pour the dressing over the pasta mixture and mix carefully. Transfer to a warmed serving bowl and serve sprinkled with fresh basil leaves.

Coconut Couscous Salad

Serves 4 • CALORIES PER SERVING: 270 • FAT CONTENT PER SERVING: 10 G

INGREDIENTS

12 ounces couscous
6 ounces dried apricots
1 small bunch fresh chives
2 tbsp unsweetened
  shredded coconut
1 tsp ground cinnamon
salt and pepper

shredded mint leaves, to
  garnish

DRESSING:
1 tbsp olive oil
2 tbsp unsweetened orange
  juice

$^1/_2$ tsp finely grated orange
  rind
1 tsp wholegrain mustard
1 tsp clear honey
2 tbsp chopped fresh mint
  leaves

1 Soak the couscous according to the instructions on the packet.

2 Bring a large pan of water to a boil. Transfer the couscous to a steamer or large strainer lined with cheesecloth and place over the water. Cover and steam as directed. Remove from the heat, place in heatproof bowl, and set aside to cool.

3 Meanwhile, slice the apricots into thin strips

and place in a small bowl. Using kitchen scissors, snip the chives over the apricots.

4 When the couscous is cool, mix in the apricots, chives, coconut, and cinnamon. Season well.

5 To make the dressing, mix all the ingredients together and season. Pour over the couscous and mix until well combined. Cover and leave to chill for 1 hour to allow the flavors to

develop. Serve the salad garnished with shredded mint leaves.

COOK'S TIP

To serve this salad hot, when the couscous has been steamed, mix in the apricots, chives, coconut, cinnamon, and seasoning, along with 1 tbsp olive oil. Transfer to a warmed serving bowl and serve.

Baking & Desserts

The ideal ending to a meal is fresh fruit,
topped with low-fat yogurt. Fruit contains no fat
and is sweet enough not to need extra sugar, but it is
a valuable source of vitamins and fiber—ideal in
every way for anyone who cares about their own
and their family's health.

There are, however, dozens of other ways
in which fruit can be used as the basis for desserts
and bakes, and thanks to modern transportation
systems, the range of unusual and exotic fruits
available in supermarkets seems to expand every
week. Experiment with some of these unfamiliar
fruits in delicious warm desserts, sophisticated
mousses and fools, and satisfying cakes, and
use old favorites in enticing new ways.

From an elegant Strawberry Roulade to add
the perfect finishing touch to a dinner party to a
deliciously moist Carrot & Ginger Cake to offer to
unexpected guests, you will find the perfect recipe for
every occasion on the following pages.

Paper-thin Fruit Pies

Serves 4 • Calories per serving: 185 • Fat content: 7.5 g

INGREDIENTS

1 medium eating apple
1 medium ripe pear
2 tbsp lemon juice
2 ounces low-fat spread

4 rectangular sheets of filo
    pastry, thawed if frozen
2 tbsp low-sugar apricot
    preserve
1 tbsp orange juice

2 tsp confectioner's sugar,
    for dusting
low-fat custard, to serve

1 Preheat the oven to 400°F. Core and thinly slice the apple and pear and toss them in the lemon juice to prevent discoloration.

2 Gently melt the low-fat spread in a pan set over a low heat.

3 Cut the sheets of pastry into 4 and cover with a clean, damp dish cloth. Brush 4 nonstick large muffin pans, measuring 4 inches across, with a little of the low-fat spread.

4 Working on each pie, separately, brush 4 sheets of pastry with low-fat spread. Press a small sheet of pastry into the base of one large muffin pan. Arrange the other sheets of pastry on top at slightly different angles. Repeat with the other sheets of pastry to make another 3 pies.

5 Arrange the apple and pear slices alternately in the center of each pastry case and lightly crimp the edges of the pastry of each pie.

6 Mix the preserve and orange juice together until smooth and brush over the fruit. Bake for 12–15 minutes. Dust lightly with confectioner's sugar, and serve hot with low-fat custard.

VARIATION

Other combinations of fruit are equally delicious. Try peach and apricot, raspberry and apple, or pineapple and mango.

Almond Trifles

Serves 4 • CALORIES PER SERVING: 230 • FAT CONTENT PER SERVING: 3.5 G

INGREDIENTS

8 Amaretti di Saronno cookies
4 tbsp brandy or Amaretto liqueur
8 ounces raspberries

$1^1/4$ cups low-fat custard
$1^1/4$ cups low-fat unsweetened yogurt
1 tsp almond extract

$^1/2$ ounce toasted almonds, slivered
1 tsp cocoa powder

1 Using the end of a rolling pin, carefully crush the cookies into small pieces.

2 Divide the crushed cookies among 4 serving glasses. Sprinkle in the brandy or liqueur and let stand for about 30 minutes to allow the cookies to soften.

3 Top the layer of cookies with a layer of raspberries, reserving a few raspberries for decoration, and spoon over enough custard to just cover.

4 Mix the unsweetened yogurt with the almond extract and spoon over the custard. Chill in the refrigerator for about 30 minutes.

5 Just before serving, sprinkle with the toasted slivered almonds and dust with a little cocoa powder. Decorate with the reserved raspberries and serve at once.

VARIATION

Try this trifle with assorted summer fruits. If they are a frozen mix, use them frozen and allow them to thaw so that the juices soak into the cookie base—it will taste delicious.

Cheese Hearts with Strawberry Sauce

Serves 4 • CALORIES PER SERVING: 120 • FAT CONTENT PER SERVING: 0.6 G

INGREDIENTS

15 1/2 ounces low-fat cottage
cheese
2/3 cup low-fat unsweetened
yogurt
1 medium egg white
2 tbsp superfine sugar

1–2 tsp vanilla extract
rose-scented geranium leaves,
to decorate (optional)

SAUCE:
8 ounces strawberries
4 tbsp unsweetened orange
juice
2–3 tsp confectioner's sugar

1 Line 4 heart-shaped molds or ramekins with clean cheesecloth. Place a strainer over a mixing bowl and using the back of a metal spoon, press the cottage cheese through. Mix in the unsweetened yogurt.

2 Whisk the egg white until stiff. Fold into the cheeses, along with the superfine sugar and vanilla extract.

3 Place the molds on a wire rack set over a baking pan. Spoon the cheese mixture into the molds and smooth over the tops. Leave to chill for 1 hour or until firm and drained.

4 Meanwhile, make the sauce. Wash the strawberries under cold running water. Reserving a few strawberries for decoration, hull and chop the remainder. Place the strawberries in a blender or food processor with the orange juice and process until smooth. Alternatively,

push through a strainer to purée. Mix with the confectioner's sugar to taste. Cover and chill until the sauce is required.

5 Remove the cheese hearts from the molds and transfer to serving plates. Remove the cheesecloth, decorate with the reserved strawberries and geranium leaves (if using), and serve with the sauce.

Almond & Raisin Cheesecakes

Serves 4 • Calories per serving: 315 • Fat content per serving: 16 g

INGREDIENTS

12 Amaretti di Saronno
  cookies
1 medium egg white, lightly
  beaten
8 ounces skimmed-milk soft
  cheese
1/2 tsp almond extract

1/2 tsp finely grated lime rind
1 ounce ground almonds
1 ounce superfine sugar
2 ounces golden raisins
2 tsp powdered gelatin
2 tbsp boiling water
2 tbsp lime juice

TO DECORATE:
1 ounces slivered toasted
  almonds
strips of lime rind

1 Preheat the oven to 350°F. Place the cookies in a clean plastic bag, seal the bag, and using a rolling pin, crush them into small pieces. Place the crumbs in a bowl and bind together with the egg white.

2 Arrange 4 nonstick pastry rings or poached egg rings, 3½ inches across, on a cookie sheet lined with baking parchment. Divide the cookie mixture into 4 equal portions and spoon it into the rings,

pressing down well. Bake for 10 minutes, until crisp, and allow to cool in the rings.

3 Beat together the soft cheese, almond extract, lime rind, ground almonds, sugar, and golden raisins until well mixed.

4 Dissolve the gelatin in the boiling water and stir in the lime juice. Fold into the cheese mixture and spoon over the cookie bases. Smooth over the tops

and chill for 1 hour, or until set.

5 Loosen the cheesecakes from the rings, using a small spatula, and transfer to serving plates. Decorate with toasted almonds and lime rind, and serve.

VARIATION

If you prefer, substitute chopped dried apricots for the golden raisins.

Red Fruits with Foaming Sauce

Serves 4 • Calories per serving: 220 • Fat content per serving: 0.3 g

INGREDIENTS

8 ounces redcurrants, washed and trimmed, thawed if frozen
8 ounces cranberries
3 ounces light brown sugar

$^3/_4$ cup unsweetened apple juice
1 cinnamon stick, broken
$10^1/_2$ ounces small strawberries, washed, hulled, and halved

SAUCE:
8 ounces raspberries, thawed if frozen
2 tbsp fruit cordial
$3^1/_2$ ounces marshmallows

1 Place the redcurrants, cranberries, and sugar in a saucepan. Pour in the apple juice and add the cinnamon stick. Bring the mixture to a boil and simmer gently for 10 minutes, until the fruit has just softened.

2 Stir the strawberries into the cranberry and sugar mixture and mix well. Transfer the mixture to a bowl, cover, and chill in the refrigerator for about 1 hour. Remove and discard the cinnamon stick.

3 Just before serving, make the sauce. Place the raspberries and fruit cordial in a small pan, bring to a boil, and simmer for 2–3 minutes, until the fruit is just beginning to soften. Stir the marshmallows into the raspberry mixture and heat through, stirring, until the marshmallows begin to melt.

4 Transfer the fruit salad to serving bowls. Top with the raspberry and marshmallow sauce and serve at once.

VARIATION

This sauce is delicious poured over low-fat ice cream. For an extra-colorful sauce, replace the raspberries with an assortment of summer berries.

Brown Bread Ice Cream

Serves 4 • CALORIES PER SERVING: 265 • FAT CONTENT PER SERVING: 6 G

INGREDIENTS

6 ounces fresh whole
    wheat bread crumbs
1 ounce finely chopped
    walnuts
2 ounces superfine sugar
1/2 tsp ground nutmeg

1 tsp finely grated orange rind
2 cups low-fat unsweetened
    yogurt
2 large egg whites

TO DECORATE:
walnut halves
orange slices
fresh mint leaves

1 Preheat the broiler. Mix the bread crumbs, walnuts, and sugar together and spread over a sheet of foil in the broiler pan. Broil, stirring frequently, for 5 minutes until crisp and evenly browned. (Take care that the sugar does not burn.) Remove from the heat and allow to cool.

2 When the mixture is cool, transfer to a mixing bowl and mix in the nutmeg, orange rind, and yogurt. In another bowl, whisk the egg whites until stiff. Gently fold the egg whites into the bread crumb mixture using a metal spoon.

3 Spoon the mixture into 4 mini-basins, smooth over the tops, and freeze for 1½–2 hours until firm.

4 To serve, hold the bases of the molds in hot water for a few seconds, then turn onto serving plates. Serve immediately, decorated with walnut halves, orange rind, and fresh mint leaves.

COOK'S TIP

If you don't have mini-basins, use ramekins or cups or, if you prefer, use one large bowl. Alternatively, spoon the mixture into a large, freezing container to freeze and serve the ice cream in scoops.

Chocolate Cheese Pots

Serves 4 • CALORIES PER SERVING: 170 • FAT CONTENT PER SERVING: 3 G

INGREDIENTS

1¼ cups low-fat ricotta
   cheese
²/₃ cup low-fat unsweetened
   yogurt
1 ounce confectioner's sugar
4 tsp low-fat drinking
   chocolate powder

4 tsp cocoa powder
1 tsp vanilla extract
2 tbsp dark rum (optional)
2 medium egg whites
4 chocolate cake decorations

TO SERVE:
pieces of kiwi fruit, orange,
   and banana
whole strawberries and
   raspberries

1   Combine the ricotta cheese and low-fat yogurt in a mixing bowl. Sift in the confectioner's sugar, chocolate powder, and cocoa powder and mix until well combined. Add the vanilla extract and rum, if using.

2   In another bowl, whisk the egg whites until stiff. Using a metal spoon, fold the egg whites into the ricotta cheese, unsweetened yogurt, and chocolate mixture.

3   Spoon the ricotta cheese, unsweetened yogurt, and chocolate mixture into 4 small china dessert pots and chill in the refrigerator for about 30 minutes. Decorate each chocolate cheese pot with a chocolate cake decoration.

4   Serve each chocolate cheese pot with an assortment of fresh fruit, such as pieces of kiwi fruit, orange, and banana, and a few whole strawberries and raspberries.

VARIATION

This chocolate mixture would make an excellent filling for a cheesecake. Make the base out of crushed Amaretti di Saronno cookies and egg white, and set the filling with 2 tsp powdered gelatin dissolved in 2 tbsp boiling water. Make sure you use cookies made from apricot kernels, which are virtually fat free.

Citrus Meringue Crush

Serves 4 • CALORIES PER SERVING: 195 • FAT CONTENT PER SERVING: 0.6 G

INGREDIENTS

8 ready-made meringue nests
1 1/4 cups low-fat natural
   unsweetened yogurt
1/2 tsp finely grated orange
   rind
1/2 tsp finely grated lemon rind
1/2 tsp finely grated lime rind
2 tbsp orange liqueur or
   unsweetened orange juice

TO DECORATE:
sliced kumquat
lime rind, grated

SAUCE:
2 ounces kumquats
8 tbsp unsweetened orange
   juice
2 tbsp lemon juice

2 tbsp lime juice
2 tbsp water
2–3 tsp superfine sugar
1 tsp cornstarch mixed with
   1 tbsp water

1 Place the meringues in a clean plastic bag, seal the bag, and using a rolling pin, crush the meringues into small pieces. Transfer to a mixing bowl.

2 Stir the yogurt, grated citrus rinds, and the liqueur or juice into the crushed meringue. Spoon the mixture into 4 mini-basins, smooth over the tops, and freeze for 1 1/2–2 hours, until firm.

3 To make the sauce, thinly slice the kumquats and place them in a pan with the fruit juices and water. Bring gently to a boil and then simmer over a low heat for 3–4 minutes, until the kumquats have just softened.

4 Sweeten with sugar to taste, stir in the cornstarch mixture, and cook, stirring, until thickened. Pour into a

small bowl, cover the surface with a layer of plastic wrap, and allow to cool—the film will help prevent a skin forming. Chill in the refrigerator.

5 To serve, dip the meringue basins in hot water for 5 seconds, or until they loosen, and turn onto serving plates. Spoon on a little sauce, decorate with slices of kumquat and lime rind, and serve.

Tropical Fruit Fool

Serves 4 • CALORIES PER SERVING: 170 • FAT CONTENT PER SERVING: 0.6 G

INGREDIENTS

1 medium ripe mango	¹/₂ tsp finely grated lime rind,	¹/₂ tsp vanilla extract
2 kiwi fruit	plus extra to decorate	2 passion fruit
1 medium banana	2 medium egg whites	
2 tbsp lime juice	15 ounce can low-fat custard	

1 To peel the mango, slice either side of the smooth, flat central pit. Roughly chop the flesh and blend the fruit in a food processor or blender until smooth. Alternatively, mash the chopped mango flesh with a fork.

2 Peel the kiwi fruit, chop the flesh into small pieces, and place in a bowl. Peel and chop the banana and add to the bowl. Toss all of the fruit in the lime juice and rind and mix well to prevent discoloration.

3 In a grease-free bowl, whisk the egg whites until stiff and then gently fold in the custard and vanilla extract until thoroughly mixed.

4 In 4 tall glasses, alternately layer the chopped fruit, mango purée, and custard mixture, finishing with the custard on top. Chill in the refrigerator for 20 minutes.

5 Halve the passion fruits, scoop out the seeds, and spoon the passion fruit over the fruit fools.

6 Decorate each serving with the extra lime rind and serve.

VARIATION

Other tropical fruits to try include papaya puree, with chopped pineapple and dates, and tamarillo or pomegranate seeds to decorate. Or make a summer fruit fool by using strawberry puree, topped with raspberries and blackberries, with cherries to finish.

Brown Sugar Pavlovas

Serves 4 • CALORIES PER SERVING: 170 • FAT CONTENT PER SERVING: 0.2 G

INGREDIENTS

2 large egg whites
1 tsp cornstarch
1 tsp raspberry vinegar
3 1/2 ounces light brown sugar, crushed free of lumps
2 tbsp redcurrant jelly

2 tbsp unsweetened orange juice
3/4 cup low-fat unsweetened yogurt
6 ounces raspberries, thawed if frozen

rose-scented geranium leaves, to decorate (optional)

1 Preheat the oven to 300°F. Line a large cookie sheet with baking parchment. In a large, grease-free bowl, whisk the egg whites until very stiff and dry. Fold in the cornstarch and vinegar.

2 Gradually whisk in the sugar, a spoonful at a time, until the mixture is thick and glossy.

3 Divide the mixture into 4 and spoon onto the cookie sheet, spaced well apart. Smooth each into a round, about 4 inches across, and bake in the oven for 40–45 minutes until lightly browned and crisp. Leave to cool on the cookie sheet.

4 Place the redcurrant jelly and orange juice in a small saucepan and heat, stirring, until the jelly has melted. Cool for 10 minutes.

5 Meanwhile, using a spatula, carefully remove each pavlova from the baking parchment and transfer to a serving plate. Top with unsweetened yogurt and raspberries. Spoon on the redcurrant jelly mixture to glaze. Decorate and serve.

VARIATION

Make a large pavlova by forming the meringue into a round, measuring 7 inches across, on a lined cookie sheet and bake for 1 hour.

Apricot & Orange Jellies

Serves 4 • CALORIES PER SERVING: 220 • FAT CONTENT PER SERVING: 4.5 G

INGREDIENTS

8 ounces no-need-to-soak
    dried apricots
1¼ cups unsweetened
    orange juice
2 tbsp lemon juice
2–3 tsp clear honey
1 tbsp powdered gelatin

4 tbsp boiling water

TO DECORATE:
orange segments
sprigs of mint

CINNAMON CREAM:
4 ounces medium fat ricotta
    cheese
4 ounces low-fat
    unsweetened yogurt
1 tsp ground cinnamon
1 tbsp clear honey

1 Place the apricots in a saucepan and pour in the orange juice. Bring to a boil, cover, and simmer for 15–20 minutes, until the apricots are plump and soft. Set aside and cool for 10 minutes.

2 Transfer the mixture to a blender or food processor and blend until smooth. Stir in the lemon juice and add the honey. Measure the mixture and make 2½ cups with cold water.

3 Dissolve the gelatin in the boiling water and stir into the apricot mixture.

4 Pour the mixture into 4 individual molds, each measuring ⅔ cup, or 1 large mold, measuring 2½ cups. Chill until set.

5 Meanwhile, make the cinnamon cream. Thoroughly mix all the ingredients together and place in a small bowl. Cover and chill.

6 To turn out the jellies, dip the molds in hot water for a few seconds to loosen, and invert onto serving plates. Decorate and serve with the cinnamon cream dusted with extra cinnamon.

VARIATION

Other fruits that would work well in this recipe instead of the apricots are dried peaches, mangoes, and pears.

Sticky Sesame Bananas

Serves 4 • CALORIES PER SERVING: 300 • FAT CONTENT PER SERVING: 4.5 G

INGREDIENTS

4 ripe medium bananas	2 tbsp sesame seeds	lemon and lime rind, shredded,
3 tbsp lemon juice	$^2/_3$ cup low-fat unsweetened	to decorate
4 ounces superfine sugar	yogurt	
4 tbsp cold water	1 tbsp confectioner's sugar	
	1 tsp vanilla extract	

1 Peel the bananas and cut into 2-inch pieces. Place the banana pieces in a bowl, add the lemon juice, and stir well to coat—this will help prevent the bananas from discoloring.

2 Place the sugar and water in a small saucepan and heat gently, stirring, until the sugar dissolves. Bring to a boil and cook for 5–6 minutes, until the mixture turns golden-brown.

3 Meanwhile, drain the bananas and blot with absorbent paper towels to dry. Line a cookie sheet or board with baking parchment and arrange the bananas, well spaced out, on top.

4 When the caramel is ready, drizzle it over the bananas, working quickly because the caramel sets almost instantly. Sprinkle with the sesame seeds and cool for about 10 minutes.

5 Mix the yogurt with the confectioner's sugar and vanilla extract.

6 Peel the bananas away from the paper and arrange on serving plates. Serve the unsweetened yogurt as a dip, decorated with the shredded lemon and lime rind.

COOK'S TIP

For the best results, use a cannelle knife or a potato peeler to peel away thin strips of rind from the fruit, taking care not to include any bitter pith. Blanch the shreds in boiling water for 1 minute, then refresh in cold water.

Mocha Swirl Mousse

Serves 4 • CALORIES PER SERVING: 130 • FAT CONTENT PER SERVING: 6.5 G

INGREDIENTS

1 tbsp coffee and chicory
extract
2 tsp cocoa powder, plus extra
for dusting
1 tsp low-fat drinking
chocolate powder

²/3 cup half-fat crème fraîche,
plus 4 tsp to serve (see
Cook's Tip)
2 tsp powdered gelatin
2 tbsp boiling water
2 large egg whites

2 tbsp superfine sugar
4 chocolate coffee beans,
to serve

1 Place the coffee and
chicory extract in one
bowl, and 2 tsp of cocoa
powder and the chocolate
powder in another bowl.
Divide the crème fraîche
between the 2 bowls and
mix both until well
combined.

2 Dissolve the gelatin in
the boiling water and
set aside. In a grease-free
bowl, whisk the egg whites
and sugar until stiff, and
divide this mixture evenly
between the coffee mixture
and the chocolate mixture.

3 Divide the dissolved
gelatin between the 2
mixtures and, using a large
metal spoon, gently fold
until well mixed.

4 Spoon small amounts
of the 2 mousses
alternately into 4 serving
glasses and swirl together
gently. Chill for 1 hour or
until set.

5 To serve, top each
mousse with 1 tsp
crème fraîche, a chocolate
coffee bean, and a light
dusting of cocoa powder.

COOK'S TIP

*Traditional crème fraîche is
sour cream and has a fat
content of around 40
percent. It is thick and has a
slightly sour and nutty
flavor. Lower-fat versions
have a reduced fat content
and are slightly looser in
texture, but they should be
used in a low-fat diet only
occasionally. If you want to
use a lower-fat alternative, a
reduced fat, unsweetened
yogurt would be
more suitable.*

Fruit & Fiber Layers

Serves 4 • CALORIES PER SERVING: 340 • FAT CONTENT PER SERVING: 6 G

INGREDIENTS

4 ounces dried apricots
4 ounces dried prunes
4 ounces dried peaches
2 ounces dried apple
1 ounce dried cherries

2 cups unsweetened apple
   juice
6 cardamom pods
6 cloves
1 cinnamon stick, broken

1¼ cups low-fat
   unsweetened yogurt
14 ounces crunchy oat cereal

TO DECORATE:
apricot slices

1 To make the fruit compote, place the dried apricots, prunes, peaches, apples, and cherries in a saucepan and pour in the apple juice.

2 Add the cardamom pods, cloves, and cinnamon stick to the pan, bring to a boil, and simmer for 10–15 minutes, until the fruits are plump and tender.

3 Allow the mixture to cool completely in the pan, then transfer the mixture to a bowl, and leave to chill in the refrigerator for 1 hour. Remove and discard the spices from the fruits.

4 Spoon the compote into 4 dessert glasses, layering it alternately with yogurt and oat cereal, finishing with the oat cereal on top.

5 Decorate each dessert with slices of apricot and serve at once.

COOK'S TIP

There are many dried fruits available, including mangoes and pears, some of which need soaking, so read the instructions on the packet before use. Also, check the ingredients label, because several types of dried fruit have added sugar, or are rolled in sugar, and this will affect the sweetness of the dish that you use them in.

Pan-cooked Apples in Red Wine

Serves 4 • CALORIES PER SERVING: 200 • FAT CONTENT PER SERVING: 4.5 G

INGREDIENTS

4 eating apples
2 tbsp lemon juice
1¹/₂ ounces low-fat spread
2 ounces light brown sugar
1 small orange

1 cinnamon stick, broken
²/₃ cup red wine
8 ounces raspberries, hulled
and thawed if frozen

sprigs of fresh mint, to
decorate

1 Peel and core the apples, then cut them into thick wedges. Place the apples in a bowl and toss in the lemon juice to prevent the fruit from discoloring.

2 In a skillet, gently melt the low-fat spread over a low heat, add the sugar, and stir to form a paste.

3 Stir the apple wedges into the skillet and cook, stirring occasionally, for 2 minutes, or until the apples are well coated in the sugar paste.

4 Using a vegetable peeler, pare off a few strips of orange rind. Add the orange rind to the pan, along with the cinnamon pieces. Extract the juice from the orange and pour into the pan with the red wine. Bring to a boil, then simmer for 10 minutes, stirring.

5 Add the raspberries to the pan and cook for 5 minutes, or until the apples are tender.

6 Discard the orange rind and cinnamon

pieces. Transfer the apple and raspberry mixture to a serving plate, together with the wine sauce. Decorate with a sprig of fresh mint and serve hot.

VARIATION

For other fruity combinations, cook the apples with blackberries, blackcurrants, or red-currants. You may need to add more sugar if you use currants, as they are not as sweet as raspberries.

Mixed Fruit Brûlées

Serves 4 • Calories per serving: 225 • Fat content per serving: 11 g

INGREDIENTS

1 pound prepared, assorted summer fruits (such as strawberries, raspberries, blackcurrants, redcurrants, and cherries), thawed if frozen	³/₄ cup half-fat heavy cream alternative ³/₄ cup low-fat unsweetened yogurt 1 tsp vanilla extract 4 tbsp raw crystal sugar

1 Divide the strawberries, raspberries, blackcurrants, redcurrants, and cherries evenly among 4 small, heatproof ramekin dishes.

2 Mix together the half-fat cream alternative, unsweetened yogurt, and vanilla extract. Generously spoon the mixture over the fruit.

3 Preheat the broiler. Top each serving with 1 tablespoon of brown crystal sugar and broil the desserts for 2–3 minutes, until the sugar melts and just begins to caramelize. Serve the fruit brûlées piping hot.

VARIATION

If you are making this dessert for a special occasion, soak the fruits in 2–3 tbsp fruit liqueur before topping with the cream mixture.

COOK'S TIP

Look for half-fat creams, in light and heavy varieties. They are good substitutes for occasional use. Alternatively, in this recipe, omit the cream and double the quantity of yogurt for a lower-fat version.

Broiled Fruit Platter with Lime "Butter"

Serves 4 • CALORIES PER SERVING: 220 • FAT CONTENT PER SERVING: 6.5 G

INGREDIENTS

1 baby pineapple	4 tbsp dark rum	LIME BUTTER:
1 ripe papaya	1 tsp ground allspice	2 ounces low-fat spread
1 ripe mango	2 tbsp lime juice	1/2 tsp finely grated lime rind
2 kiwi fruit	4 tbsp dark brown sugar	1 tbsp confectioner's sugar
4 finger bananas		

1 Quarter the pineapple, trimming away most of the leaves, and place in a shallow dish. Peel the papaya, cut it in half, and scoop out the seeds. Cut the flesh into thick wedges and place in the same dish as the pineapple.

2 Peel the mango, cut either side of the smooth, central flat pit and remove the pit. Slice the flesh into thick wedges. Peel the kiwi fruit and cut in half. Peel the bananas. Add all of these fruits to the dish.

3 Sprinkle with the rum, allspice, and lime juice, cover, and leave at room temperature for about 30 minutes, turning occasionally, to allow the flavors to develop.

4 Meanwhile, make the lime butter. Place the low-fat spread in a small bowl and beat in the lime rind and sugar until well mixed. Chill until the butter is required.

5 Preheat the broiler. Drain the fruit, reserving the juices, and arrange in the broiler pan. Sprinkle with the sugar and broil for 3–4 minutes until hot and just beginning to char.

6 Transfer the fruit to a serving plate and spoon the juices on top. Serve the fruit with the lime butter.

VARIATION

Serve with a light sauce of 1 1/4 cups tropical fruit juice thickened with 2 tsp arrowroot.

Baked Pears with Cinnamon & Brown Sugar

Serves 4 • CALORIES PER SERVING: 160 • FAT CONTENT PER SERVING: 6 G

INGREDIENTS

4 ripe pears	1 tsp ground cinnamon	lemon rind, finely grated, to
2 tbsp lemon juice	2 ounces low-fat spread	decorate
4 tbsp light brown sugar	low-fat custard, to serve	

1 Preheat the oven to 400°F. Core and peel the pears, then slice them in half lengthwise, and brush all over with the lemon juice to prevent the pears from discoloring. Place the pears, cored side down, in a small nonstick roasting pan.

2 Place the sugar, cinnamon, and low-fat spread in a small saucepan and heat gently, stirring, until the sugar has melted. Keep the heat low to stop too much water evaporating from the low-fat spread as it gets hot. Spoon the mixture over the pears.

3 Bake in the oven for 20–25 minutes, or until the pears are tender and golden, occasionally spooning the sugar mixture over the fruit during the cooking time.

4 To serve, heat the custard until it is piping hot and spoon over the bases of 4 warm dessert plates. Arrange 2 pear halves on each plate. Decorate and serve.

VARIATION

This recipe also works well if you use cooking apples. For alternative flavors, replace the cinnamon with ground ginger, and serve the pears sprinkled with chopped, preserved ginger in syrup. Alternatively, use ground allspice and spoon warm dark rum on top.

Baked Apples with Blackberries

Serves 4 • CALORIES PER SERVING: 250 • FAT CONTENT PER SERVING: 2 G

INGREDIENTS

4 medium-size cooking apples	$^1/_2$ tsp finely grated lemon rind	low-fat custard, to serve
1 tbsp lemon juice	2 tbsp raw crystal sugar	
$3^1/_2$ ounces prepared blackberries, thawed if frozen	$1^1/_4$ cups ruby port	
$^1/_2$ ounce slivered almonds	1 cinnamon stick, broken	
$^1/_2$ tsp ground allspice	2 tsp cornstarch blended with 2 tbsp cold water	

1 Preheat the oven to 400°F. Wash and dry the apples. Using a small sharp knife, make a shallow cut through the skin around the middle of each apple—this will help the apples to cook through.

2 Core the apples, brush the centers with the lemon juice to prevent browning, and stand in a shallow ovenproof dish.

3 In a bowl, mix together the blackberries, almonds, allspice, lemon rind, and sugar. Using a teaspoon, spoon the mixture into the center of each apple.

4 Pour the port into the dish, add the cinnamon stick, and bake the apples in the oven for 35–40 minutes, or until tender. Drain the cooking juices into a pan and keep the apples warm.

5 Discard the cinnamon and add the cornstarch mixture to the cooking juices. Heat, stirring, until thickened.

6 Heat the custard until piping hot. Pour the sauce over the apples and serve with the custard.

VARIATION

Use raspberries instead of blackberries and, if you prefer, replace the port with unsweetened orange juice.

White Lace Crêpes with Oriental Fruits

Serves 4 • CALORIES PER SERVING: 170 • FAT CONTENT PER SERVING: 1.5 G

INGREDIENTS

3 medium egg whites	FRUIT FILLING:	¹/₂-inch piece fresh root ginger
4 tbsp cornstarch	12 ounces fresh lychees	2 pieces preserved ginger in
3 tbsp cold water	¹/₄ Galia melon	syrup
1 tsp vegetable oil	6 ounces seedless green grapes	2 tbsp ginger wine or dry sherry

1 To make the fruit filling, peel the lychees and remove the pits. Place the lychees in a bowl. Scoop out the seeds from the melon and remove the skin. Cut the melon flesh into small pieces and place in the bowl.

2 Wash and dry the grapes, remove from the stalks, and add to the bowl. Peel the ginger root and cut into thin shreds or grate finely. Drain the preserved ginger pieces, reserving the syrup, and chop the ginger finely.

3 Mix the gingers into the bowl, along with the ginger wine or sherry and the reserved preserved ginger syrup. Cover and set aside.

4 Meanwhile, prepare the crêpes. In a small pitcher, mix together the egg whites, cornstarch, and cold water until very smooth.

5 Brush a small nonstick crêpe pan with oil and heat until hot. Drizzle the surface of the pan with a quarter of the cornstarch

mixture to give a lacy effect. Cook for a few seconds until set, then carefully lift out, and transfer to absorbent paper towels to drain. Set aside and keep warm. Repeat with the remaining mixture to make 4 crêpes in total.

6 To serve, place a crêpe on each serving plate and top with the fruit filling. Fold over the pancake and serve hot.

Fruit Loaf with Strawberry & Apple Spread

Serves 8 • CALORIES PER SERVING: 360 • FAT CONTENT PER SERVING: 2.8 G

INGREDIENTS

6 ounces oatmeal
3 1/2 ounces light brown sugar
1 tsp ground cinnamon
4 1/2 ounces golden raisins
6 ounces seedless raisins
2 tbsp malt extract
1 1/4 cups unsweetened apple
  juice

6 ounces self-rising whole
  wheat flour
1 1/2 tsp baking powder
strawberries and apple wedges,
  to serve

FRUIT SPREAD:
8 ounces strawberries, washed
  and hulled

2 eating apples, cored,
  chopped, and mixed with
  1 tbsp lemon juice to
  prevent browning
1 1/4 cups unsweetened apple
  juice

1 Preheat the oven to 350°F. Grease and line a 2-pound loaf pan. Place the oatmeal, sugar, cinnamon, golden raisins, raisins, and malt extract in a mixing bowl. Pour in the apple juice, stir well, and let soak for 30 minutes.

2 Sift in the flour and baking powder, adding any husks that remain in the strainer, and fold in using a metal spoon. Spoon the mixture into the pan and bake for 1½ hours, until firm or until a skewer inserted into the center comes out clean. Cool for 10 minutes, then turn onto a rack, and cool completely.

3 Meanwhile, make the fruit spread. Place the strawberries and apples in a saucepan and pour in the apple juice. Bring to a boil, cover, and simmer for 30 minutes. Beat the sauce well and spoon into a clean, warmed jar. Set aside and let cool, then seal the jar.

4 Serve the loaf with 1–2 tablespoons of the fruit spread and an assortment of strawberries and apple wedges.

Banana & Lime Cake

Serves 10 • CALORIES PER SERVING: 360 • FAT CONTENT PER SERVING: 2.8 G

INGREDIENTS

10$\frac{1}{2}$ ounces all-purpose flour
1 tsp salt
1$\frac{1}{2}$ tsp baking powder
6 ounces light brown sugar
1 tsp lime rind, grated
1 medium egg, beaten
1 medium banana, mashed
   with 1 tbsp lime juice

$\frac{2}{3}$ cup low-fat unsweetened
   yogurt
4 ounces golden raisins

TOPPING:
4 ounces confectioner's sugar
1–2 tsp lime juice
$\frac{1}{2}$ tsp lime rind, finely grated

TO DECORATE:
banana chips
lime rind, finely grated

1 Preheat the oven to 350°F. Grease and line a deep 7-inch round cake pan with baking parchment. Sift the flour, salt, and baking powder into a mixing bowl and stir in the sugar and lime rind until well combined.

2 Make a well in the center of the dry ingredients and add the egg, banana, yogurt, and golden raisins. Mix until thoroughly incorporated.

3 Spoon the mixture into the pan and smooth the surface. Bake for 40–45 minutes, until firm to the touch or until a skewer inserted in the center comes out clean. Cool for 10 minutes, then turn out onto a wire rack.

4 To make the topping, sift the confectioner's sugar into a small bowl and mix with the lime juice to form a soft, but not too runny, frosting. Stir in the lime rind. Drizzle the frosting over the cake, letting it run down the sides.

5 Decorate with banana chips and lime rind. Let stand for 15 minutes, so that the frosting sets.

VARIATION

Replace the lime rind and juice with orange, and the golden raisins with chopped apricots, if preferred.

Crispy Sugar-topped Blackberry & Apple Cake

Serves 10 • CALORIES PER SERVING: 230 • FAT CONTENT PER SERVING: 1.5 G

INGREDIENTS

12 ounces cooking apples
3 tbsp lemon juice
10 1/2 ounces self-rising whole wheat flour
1/2 tsp baking powder
1 tsp ground cinnamon, plus extra for dusting

6 ounces prepared blackberries, thawed if frozen, plus extra to decorate
6 ounces light brown sugar
1 medium egg, beaten
3/4 cup low-fat unsweetened yogurt

2 ounces white or brown sugar cubes, lightly crushed
sliced eating apple, to decorate

1 Preheat the oven to 375°F. Grease and line a 2-pound loaf pan. Core, peel, and finely dice the apples. Place them in a saucepan with the lemon juice, bring to a boil, cover, and simmer for 10 minutes, until soft and pulpy. Beat well and set aside to cool.

2 Sift the flour, baking powder, and 1 tsp cinnamon into a bowl, adding any husks that remain in the strainer. Stir in 4 ounces blackberries and the sugar.

3 Make a well in the center of the ingredients and add the egg, unsweetened yogurt, and cooled apple purée. Mix well to incorporate thoroughly. Spoon the mixture into the prepared loaf pan and smooth over the top.

4 Sprinkle with the blackberries, pressing them down into the mixture, and top with the crushed sugar. Bake for 40–45 minutes. Cool in the pan.

5 Remove the cake from the pan and peel away the lining paper. Serve dusted with cinnamon.

Rich Fruit Cake

Serves 12 • CALORIES PER SERVING: 315 • FAT CONTENT PER SERVING: 3 G

INGREDIENTS

6 ounces unsweetened pitted
   dates
4 ounces dried prunes
³/4 cup unsweetened orange
   juice
2 tbsp molasses
1 tsp finely grated lemon rind
1 tsp finely grated orange rind

8 ounces self-rising whole
   wheat flour
1 tsp apple pie spice
4 ounces seedless raisins
4 ounces golden sultanas
4 ounces currants
4 ounces dried cranberries
3 large eggs, separated
confectioner's sugar, to dust

TO DECORATE:
1 tbsp apricot preserves,
   softened
6 ounces sugar paste
strips of orange rind
strips of lemon rind

1 Preheat the oven to
325°F. Grease and line a
deep 8-inch round cake pan.
Chop the dates and prunes
and place in a pan. Add the
orange juice and bring to a
boil. Simmer for 10 minutes
until soft. Remove from the
heat and beat the mixture
until puréed. Stir in the
molasses and citrus rinds
until combined. Let cool.

2 Sift the flour and apple
pie spice into a bowl,
adding any husks that
remain in the strainer. Mix
in the dried fruits.

3 When the date and
prune mixture is cool,
whisk in the egg yolks. In
a separate bowl, whisk the
egg whites until stiff.
Spoon the fruit and egg
yolk mixture into the dry
ingredients, and mix.

4 Gently fold in the egg
whites, using a metal
spoon. Transfer to the pan
and bake for 1½ hours.
Cool completely in the pan.

5 Remove the cake from
the pan and brush the
top with preserves. Dust
the counter with
confectioner's sugar and
roll out the sugar paste
thinly. Lay the sugar paste
over the top of the cake and
trim the edges. Decorate
the cake with orange and
lemon rind.

Carrot & Ginger Cake

Serves 10 • CALORIES PER SERVING: 300 • FAT CONTENT PER SERVING: 10 G

INGREDIENTS

8 ounces all-purpose flour
1 tsp baking powder
1 tsp baking soda
2 tsp ground ginger
$1/2$ tsp salt
6 ounces light brown sugar
8 ounces carrots, grated
2 pieces of preserved ginger in
    syrup, drained and
    chopped

1 ounce fresh ginger root,
    grated
2 ounces seedless raisins
2 medium eggs, beaten
3 tbsp corn oil
juice of 1 medium orange

FROSTING:
8 ounces low-fat soft cheese
4 tbsp confectioner's sugar

1 tsp vanilla extract

TO DECORATE:
grated carrot
preserved ginger
ground ginger

1 Preheat the oven to 350°F. Grease and line an 8-inch round cake pan with baking parchment.

2 Sift the flour, baking powder, baking soda, ground ginger, and salt into a mixing bowl. Stir in the sugar, carrots, preserved ginger, fresh root ginger, and raisins. Make a well in the center of the dry ingredients.

3 Beat together the eggs, oil, and orange juice, then pour into the center of the well. Combine until well mixed.

4 Spoon the mixture into the pan and smooth the surface. Bake in the oven for 1–1¼ hours, until firm to the touch, or until a skewer inserted into the center comes out clean. Cool in the pan.

5 To make the frosting, place the soft cheese in a bowl and beat to soften. Sift in the confectioner's sugar and add the vanilla extract. Stir until combined.

6 Remove the cake from the pan and smooth the frosting over the top. Serve decorated with grated carrot, preserved ginger, and a dusting of ground ginger.

Strawberry Roulade

Serves 8 • CALORIES PER SERVING: 185 • FAT CONTENT PER SERVING: 4 G

INGREDIENTS

3 large eggs
4 ounces superfine sugar
4 ounces all-purpose flour
1 tbsp hot water

FILLING:
$3/4$ cup low-fat unsweetened
  yogurt
1 tsp almond extract
8 ounces small strawberries

$1/2$ ounce toasted
  almonds, slivered
1 tsp confectioner's sugar

1 Preheat the oven to 425°F. Line a 14 × 10-inch jelly roll pan with baking parchment. Place the eggs in a mixing bowl with the superfine sugar. Place the bowl over a pan of hot water and whisk until pale and thick.

2 Remove the bowl from the pan. Sift in the flour and fold into the eggs with the hot water. Pour the mixture into the pan and bake for 8–10 minutes, until golden and set.

3 Transfer the mixture to a sheet of baking parchment. Peel off the lining paper and roll up the sponge tightly along with the baking parchment. Wrap in a dish cloth and let cool.

4 To make the filling, mix together the yogurt and almond extract. Reserving a few strawberries for decoration, wash, hull, and slice the rest. Leave the filling mixture to chill until ready to assemble.

5 Unroll the sponge, spread the yogurt mixture over the sponge, and sprinkle with strawberries. Roll the sponge up again and transfer to a serving plate. Sprinkle with the almonds and dust with confectioner's sugar. Decorate with the reserved strawberries.

VARIATION

Serve the roulade with a fruit puree, sweetened with a little sugar.

Fruity Muffins

Makes 10 • CALORIES PER SERVING: 180 • FAT CONTENT PER SERVING: 1.5 G

INGREDIENTS

8 ounces self-rising whole
    wheat flour
2 tsp baking powder
1 ounce light muscovado
    sugar
3 1/2 ounces dried apricots,
    finely chopped

1 medium banana, mashed
    with 1 tbsp orange juice
1 tsp orange rind, grated
    finely
1 1/4 cups skim milk
1 medium egg, beaten

3 tbsp corn oil
2 tbsp oatmeal
fruit spread, honey, or maple
    syrup, to serve

1 Preheat the oven to 400°F. Place 10 paper muffin cups in a deep muffin pan.

2 Sift the flour and baking powder into a mixing bowl, adding any husks that remain in the strainer. Stir in the sugar and chopped apricots and mix until well combined.

3 Make a well in the center of the dry ingredients and add the banana, orange rind, milk, beaten egg, and oil. Mix well to form a thick batter. Divide the batter evenly among the 10 paper cups.

4 Sprinkle with a little oatmeal and bake for 25–30 minutes, until well risen and firm to the touch, or until a toothpick inserted into the center comes out clean. Transfer the muffins to a wire rack to cool slightly.

5 Serve the muffins warm with fruit spread, honey, or maple syrup.

VARIATION

If you like dried figs, they make a deliciously crunchy alternative to the apricots; they also go very well with the flavor of orange. Other no-need-to-soak dried fruits, chopped up finely, can be used as well. Store these muffins in an airtight container for 3-4 days. They also freeze well in sealed bags or in freezer containers for up to 3 months.

Chocolate Brownies

Makes 12 • CALORIES PER SERVING: 300 • FAT CONTENT PER SERVING: 4.5 G

INGREDIENTS

2 ounces unsweetened pitted dates, chopped

2 ounces dried prunes, chopped

6 tbsp unsweetened apple juice

4 medium eggs, beaten

10 1/2 ounces dark brown sugar

1 tsp vanilla extract

4 tbsp low-fat drinking chocolate powder, plus extra for dusting

2 tbsp cocoa powder

6 ounces all-purpose flour

2 ounces dark chocolate chips

FROSTING:

4 ounces confectioner's sugar

1–2 tsp water

1 tsp vanilla extract

1 Preheat the oven to 350°F. Grease and line a 7 × 11-inch cake pan with baking parchment. Place the dates and prunes in a small saucepan and add the apple juice. Bring to a boil, cover, and simmer for 10 minutes, until soft. Beat to form a smooth paste, then set aside to cool.

2 Place the cooled fruit in a mixing bowl and stir in the eggs, sugar, and vanilla extract. Sift in 4 tablespoons of chocolate powder, the cocoa, and the flour, and fold in, along with the chocolate chips, until well incorporated.

3 Spoon the mixture into the prepared pan and smooth over the top. Bake for 25–30 minutes until firm to the touch or until a toothpick inserted into the center of the cake comes out clean. Cut into 12 bars and cool in the pan for 10 minutes. Transfer the brownies to a wire rack to cool completely.

4 To make the frosting, sift the sugar into a bowl and mix with enough water and the vanilla extract to form a soft, but not too runny, frosting.

5 Drizzle the frosting over the chocolate brownies and allow to set. Dust with the extra chocolate powder just before serving.

Cheese & Chive Biscuits

Makes 10 • CALORIES PER SERVING: 120 • FAT CONTENT PER SERVING: 2.8 G

INGREDIENTS

9 ounces self-rising flour
1 tsp powdered mustard
$\frac{1}{2}$ tsp cayenne pepper
$\frac{1}{2}$ tsp salt

$3\frac{1}{2}$ ounces low-fat soft
cheese with added herbs
2 tbsp fresh snipped chives,
plus extra to garnish

$3\frac{1}{2}$ fl ounces and 2 tbsp
skim milk
2 ounces reduced-fat vheddar
cheese, grated
low-fat soft cheese, to serve

1 Preheat the oven to 400°F. Sift the self-rising flour, mustard, cayenne pepper, and salt into a mixing bowl.

2 Add the soft cheese to the mixture and mix together until well incorporated. Stir in the snipped chives.

3 Make a well in the center of the ingredients and gradually pour in 3½ fl ounces milk, stirring as you pour, until the mixture forms a soft dough.

4 Turn the dough onto a floured counter and knead lightly. Roll out until $\frac{3}{4}$ inch thick and use a 2-inch plain pastry cutter to stamp out as many rounds as you can. Transfer the rounds to a cookie sheet.

5 Re-knead the dough trimmings together and roll out again. Stamp out more rounds—you should be able to make 10 biscuits in total.

6 Brush the biscuits with the remaining milk and sprinkle with the grated cheese. Bake for 15–20 minutes, until risen and golden. Transfer to a wire rack to cool. Serve warm with low-fat soft cheese, garnished with chives.

VARIATION

For a sweet variation omit the mustard, cayenne, chives, and grated cheese and add 3 ounces currants or raisins and 1 ounce sugar, and use plain low-fat soft cheese.

Savory Tomato & Bell Pepper Bread

Serves 8 • Calories per serving: 250 • Fat content per serving: 3 g

INGREDIENTS

1 small red bell pepper

1 small green bell pepper

1 small yellow bell pepper

2 ounces dry-pack sun-dried tomatoes

$1/4$ cup boiling water

2 tsp dried yeast

1 tsp superfine sugar

$2/3$ cup tepid water

4 cups strong white bread flour

2 tsp dried rosemary

2 tbsp tomato paste

$2/3$ cup low-fat unsweetened yogurt

1 tbsp coarse salt

1 tbsp olive oil

1 Preheat the oven to 425°F and the broiler to hot. Halve and seed the bell peppers, arrange on the broiler rack, and cook until the skin is charred. Cool for 10 minutes, peel off the skin, and chop the flesh.

2 Slice the tomatoes into strips, place in a heatproof bowl, and add the boiling water. Let soak.

3 Place the yeast and sugar in a small pitcher, add the water, and

leave for 10–15 minutes, until frothy. Sift the flour into a bowl and add 1 tsp dried rosemary. Make a well in the center and pour in the yeast mixture. Add the tomato paste, the tomatoes and soaking liquid, the bell peppers, yogurt, and half the salt. Mix together to form a soft dough.

4 Knead the dough on a floured counter for 3–4 minutes, until smooth and elastic. Place in a floured

bowl, cover, and leave in a warm room for 40 minutes, until doubled in size. Knead the dough again and place in a greased, 9-inch round, spring-form cake pan. Using a wooden spoon, form "dimples" in the surface. Cover and leave for 30 minutes.

5 Brush with oil and sprinkle with rosemary and salt. Bake for 35–40 minutes, cool, and release from the pan.

Index

Index compiled by Hilary Bird.